The Way
I Cook...

LISA FAULKNER

The Way I Cook...

SIMON &
SCHUSTER
ILLUSTRATED

London · New York · Sydney · Toronto · New Delhi

A CBS COMPANY

First published in Great Britain in 2013
by Simon & Schuster UK Ltd
A CBS Company

10 9 8 7 6 5 4 3 2 1

Simon & Schuster Illustrated Books
Simon & Schuster UK Ltd
222 Gray's Inn Road
London
WC1X 8HB

www.simonandschuster.co.uk

Simon & Schuster Australia, Sydney
Simon & Schuster India, New Delhi

A CIP catalogue record for this book is available
from the British Library

ISBN 978-0-85720-618-3

Senior Commissioning Editor: Nicky Hill
Project Editor: Abi Waters
Designer: Miranda Harvey
Photographer: Chris Terry
Home Economist: Richard Harris
Stylist: Polly Webb-Wilson
Hair and Make-up: Justine Wade
Director of Illustrated Publishing: Ami Richards
Production Manager: Katherine Thornton

Colour reproduction by Dot Gradations Ltd, UK
Printed and bound in China

Notes on the recipes

Both metric and imperial measurements have been given in all recipes. Use one set of measurements only and not a mixture of both.

Spoon measures are level and 1 tablespoon = 15 ml, 1 teaspoon = 5 ml.

Recipe ingredients can be changed and are not set in stone, but please be aware that this might affect cooking times and results.

Preheat ovens before use and cook on the centre shelf wherever possible. If using a fan oven, reduce the heat by 10–20°C, but check with your handbook.

Medium free-range eggs have been used unless otherwise stated in the recipes.

Salt and freshly ground black pepper used throughout unless otherwise stated.

I tend to use unsalted butter and light olive oil in my cooking, but use whichever sort you normally use.

This book contains recipes made with nuts. Those with known allergic reactions to nuts and nut derivatives, pregnant and breast-feeding women and very young children should avoid these dishes.

Also by Lisa Faulkner
and published by Simon & Schuster Illustrated

ISBN 978-0-85720-617-6

Contents

The way I cook... 6

Basic recipes 8

The Way I Cook...

The Way I Cook...

It's funny writing a second book – there's quite a bit of pressure, especially when the first one did so well… it's sort of looked upon as that 'difficult second album'. Except in this case, I had this idea and couldn't wait to get started, so for me it didn't really seem like that.

Cooking is everything to me – it calms me and it anchors me. Whenever life throws its curve balls, I instantly gravitate towards the kitchen. I can hide in recipe books and in food memories. There's something about measuring, weighing, chopping and tasting that sorts me right out!

I also find that I want to cook different things at different times – a song on the radio, a family photo, a conversation with my friends, a picture in a magazine and, most importantly, the weather can change the way I feel and ultimately the way I cook, and I wanted to share this.

The book is divided into chapters, with some that make more sense than others. For instance, '…For Family and Friends' is pretty self-explanatory but '…On Rainy Days' isn't necessarily about comfort food on cold days; it's about locking myself away and cheering myself up in the best way I know how. And '…When the Sun is Shining' works both ways I think – it does exactly what it says on the tin, but it's also good if you wanted to inject a little of that sunshine into a dark day!

I really hope that you enjoy this book as much as I have enjoyed writing it. Feel free to use it in whatever way you like, using different recipes for different times. It is very personal to me, hence *The Way I Cook...*, but somehow I think I'm not alone ;)

Enjoy!

Lisa xxx

Basic recipes

The following recipes are just a small selection of basic pastries, pasta, bread and sauces that I think are handy for all kinds of cooking. The pastries obviously are great for baking and are used in a number of recipes later on in the book. Likewise with the sauces – but feel free to use any of these basic recipes for other dishes as you see fit.

FLAKY PASTRY

I love this pastry as it's in between puff and shortcrust. Crumbly and buttery and delicious.

MAKES ENOUGH FOR A 23 CM
(9 INCH) PIE

150 g (5 oz) plain flour

a pinch of salt

100 g (3½ oz) unsalted butter, chilled and cubed

3 tablespoons iced water

Note: If you have a food processor or stand mixer it is the easiest way, but if not you can do this by hand in a large bowl, but use a knife to combine and touch the pastry as little as possible.

Tip the flour, salt and cubed butter into a food processor (see Note about making by hand) and pulse until you get a coarse breadcrumb mixture. Add the water and pulse again until the mixture just comes together – but stop before it forms a ball.

Turn the dough out on to some greaseproof paper and flatten into a disc. Put another sheet of greaseproof over the top and use a rolling pin to roll it a little flatter. Scrunch up the sides of the paper to seal the dough inside and then leave it to rest in the fridge for at least an hour before rolling out and using for baking a pie or tart.

ROUGH PUFF PASTRY

Shop-bought puff pastry really is great, but I like the ritual that goes into making this... it's great for sausage rolls!

MAKES ENOUGH FOR A 23 CM
(9 INCH) PIE

225 g (7½ oz) plain flour, plus
extra for dusting

a pinch of salt

225 g (7½ oz) very cold butter,
chopped into 2.5 cm (1 inch)
cubes

150 ml (¼ pint) ice-cold water

Sift the flour and salt into a large bowl. Add the cold cubed butter, tossing it through to coat but not really rubbing it in. Add the water slowly and mix with a knife until it comes together as a stiff dough. The butter should still be in chunks at this stage. Wrap the dough in cling film and chill for about 20–30 minutes.

On a floured surface, roll the dough out to form a rectangle. Fold the top down two-thirds of the way and bring the bottom third up to cover it. Give the dough a quarter turn to the right and roll out into a rectangle again. Repeat the process 3 times so that all the butter is incorporated into the dough. Rest in the fridge for at least 30 minutes before using.

SHORTCRUST PASTRY

This is a great basic pastry for pretty much anything, sweet or savoury.

MAKES ENOUGH FOR A 23 CM
(9 INCH) PIE

375 g (12 oz) plain flour

125 g (4 oz) cold lard, cubed

50 g (2 oz) cold margarine,
cubed

a pinch of salt

1–2 tablespoons cold water

Put the flour, lard, margarine and salt in a food processor or stand mixer and pulse until the mixture resembles fine breadcrumbs.

Add the cold water and pulse again until a dough is formed.

Shape into a round dough, wrap in cling film and chill for 30 minutes before using.

PASTA

Making pasta dough from scratch is so worth the effort – you can really taste the difference – and I get huge satisfaction from knowing I have made it myself. You will need a pasta machine to make this recipe.

MAKES ABOUT 250 G (8 OZ)

200 g (7 oz) '00' pasta flour, plus extra for dusting

a pinch of salt

2 eggs

2 egg yolks

Sift the flour and salt into a large bowl and then tip into the bowl of a food processor with the eggs and yolks. Blitz for a few seconds until the mixture resembles breadcrumbs and then tip out on to a lightly floured work surface. Using your hands, bring the mixture together to form a ball of dough and then knead for 5 minutes until smooth and firm. Cut the dough in two; wrap each half in cling film and rest in the fridge for 1 hour before rolling.

Set the pasta machine to its thickest setting. Unwrap one ball of dough and roll out into a rough rectangle with a rolling pin. Pass the dough through the machine twice and then change to the second setting.

Pass the dough through the machine again and then fold the ends of the sheet in to meet in the middle. Turn the pasta through 90 degrees and pass back through the machine. Repeat this 3 times until the pasta is smooth, shiny and streak-free. Try not to use any flour to dust the machine or pasta as this can dry the dough and cause it to tear or crack.

FLATBREADS

These easy flatbreads are a great addition to any simple Greek-style lamb dish.

MAKES 12 GOOD-SIZE BREADS

500 g (1 lb) plain flour

1 teaspoon salt

1 teaspoon sugar

1 teaspoon fresh yeast

100 ml (3½ fl oz) milk

150 ml (¼ pint) natural yogurt

60 g (2¼ oz) clarified butter
or ghee

Put the flour, salt, sugar and yeast in a large bowl and mix well. Heat the milk until lukewarm. Reserving 1 tablespoon of the yogurt, add the rest to the milk, blending thoroughly. Melt the butter and add to the milk and yogurt, mixing well.

Pour slowly over the flour and mix together, then knead until you have a springy dough. Leave the dough to rise in a warm place for about 1 hour, until doubled in size. Divide the dough into 10 even-sized balls, cover and leave for about 15 minutes. Preheat a a moderate grill and put a large baking tray under it to heat for about 10 minutes.

Flatten the balls of dough into rough teardrop shapes and spread with the reserved yogurt. Place on the hot baking tray and grill under moderate heat for about 2–3 minutes on each side until golden. Keep a close eye on the flatbreads as they can burn very quickly.

SOURDOUGH STARTER

This starter will make all the difference to your sourdough loaf (see page 92).

MAKES ENOUGH STARTER TO
MAKE 2 LOAVES AND SOME
LEFT OVER

150ml (¼ pint) skimmed milk

75 ml (3 fl oz) natural yogurt

270 g (9 oz) white flour

150 ml (¼ pint) water

Note: If by the end of Day 6 your starter is not as active as hoped, don't worry – simply repeat the feeding process of Day 5 and allow an extra 12–24 hours.

Day 1: Heat the milk gently in a saucepan. Put the yogurt in a bowl and add the warm milk. Cover and leave in a warm place for 12–24 hours until thickened. Stir.

Day 2: Stir 125 g (4 oz) of the flour into the yogurt mixture, mixing evenly. Cover and leave in a warm place for 2 days. The mixture should be full of bubbles and smell pleasantly sour.

Day 5: Add the remaining flour to the starter and mix in the water. Cover and leave in a warm place for 12–24 hours.

Day 6: The starter should be quite active now and be full of little bubbles.

Feed the starter once a week with an equal amount of flour and water (about 1 cup of each) if you are baking regularly and keep stored in a sealed airtight container.

RED WINE & CHOCOLATE SAUCE

A deliciously rich sauce that goes perfectly with venison (see page 166) or other red meats, like lamb or beef.

SERVES 4

olive oil, for frying

2 shallots, peeled and chopped

2 garlic cloves, crushed

2 thyme sprigs

1 bay leaf

1 teaspoon juniper berries, crushed

1 teaspoon black peppercorns, crushed

300 ml (½ pint) red wine

200 ml (7 fl oz) dark chicken stock

4 squares of dark chocolate, grated

25 g (1 oz) cold unsalted butter

a pinch of salt

Heat a splash of olive oil in a saucepan over a medium heat. Add the shallots and garlic and fry for 5 minutes until they start to caramelise.

Add the herbs, juniper berries and peppercorns and fry for a further 2 minutes until fragrant. Pour in the wine, bring to the boil and simmer until reduced by two-thirds. Add the chicken stock and simmer until reduced by half. Strain the sauce into a clean saucepan and keep warm.

Just before serving, remove the sauce from the heat and whisk in the chocolate and butter and season with a pinch of salt.

CREAMY GRAVY

This is the perfect gravy recipe to accompany any roast meat dish – you will need to use some of the fat or oil from the roasting pan.

SERVES 4

3 tablespoons fat/oil from your roasting pan

3 tablespoons plain flour

250 ml (9 fl oz) whole milk

salt

Heat the fat/oil from your roasting pan in a saucepan set over a medium heat and stir in the flour. Cook until bubbling, but not browned. Gradually stir in the milk, add salt to taste and then cook until thick and creamy.

BÉCHAMEL SAUCE

This is a great base white sauce, ideal for lasagne and fish. Add cheese, mustard powder, herbs… whatever you wish.

MAKES ABOUT 600 ML (1 PINT)
50 g (2 oz) butter
50 g (2 oz) plain flour
1 onion, cut in half at root
2 cloves
3 peppercorns
1 bay leaf
600 ml (1 pint) milk

Put the butter in a saucepan over a medium heat. When the butter has melted, add the flour and stir to make a roux. Make sure you cook out the flour otherwise the sauce will taste floury.

Pierce the onion halves with the cloves and put in a separate pan with the peppercorns, bay leaf and milk. Heat slowly over a low heat. When the milk is lukewarm, strain it little by little into the roux (discarding the onion halves, peppercorns and bay leaf), stirring all the time over a medium-low heat. Keep adding and stirring until all the milk has been used and the sauce has thickened.

MYSTIC PIZZA TOMATO SAUCE

The Mystic tomato sauce used for their pizzas and meatballs is a closely guarded secret. However, when I visited the famous restaurant in America I was lucky enough to discover the mystery ingredients – this is my take on their well-known sauce.

SERVES 4
1 x 400 g tin chopped tomatoes
2 garlic cloves, crushed
1 heaped teaspoon freshly chopped basil
1 heaped teaspoon freshly chopped mint
½ dessertspoon freshly chopped oregano
½ teaspoon sugar
salt and pepper

Note: Feel free to add more or fewer herbs to taste.

Put all the ingredients in a saucepan over a medium heat. Bring to the boil and continue to cook and reduce until the mixture thickens to a pizza sauce consistency.

Use on top of fresh pasta (see page 10) or pizza, or with meat dishes of your choice.

for Family & Friends

I decided to buy my house because I fell in love with the kitchen –
it's large enough to fit a lot of people; it's bright,
with doors opening out on to the garden, and
above all I can cook and chat all at the same time.
Dinner parties aren't really what they used to be
when my parents had them, but the excitement
of making something special is still alive and well.
Usually dinner parties are decided that day, friends
or family bringing round different dishes; not
enough chairs around the table so they have to
be found elsewhere; mismatching crockery; the
garden table brought in from outside, and again,
noise! We have an expression we use a lot: 'We eat
like kings' – and we really do. We eat enough to
feed small armies and by the end of the night there
is usually nothing left.

I made this once when I wanted a big plate of pie and nothing else! I had a packet of stuffing mix and thought it would be lovely to incorporate it into the pastry. Feel free to make this as quick or as time consuming as you like – I used ready-rolled puff pastry and ready-made stuffing mix. It makes a great family dinner using up leftover roast chicken.

Chicken pie with stuffing pastry

SERVES 4–6

1 x 170 g pack sage and onion stuffing mix

100 g (3½ oz) butter

1 onion, thinly sliced

50 g (2 oz) plain flour, plus extra for dusting

200 ml (7 fl oz) chicken stock

125 ml (4 fl oz) single cream

500–600 g (1 lb–1 lb 3 oz) cooked chicken (the meat from a cooked chicken or about 4 chicken breasts)

200 g (7 oz) mushrooms, sliced

2 tablespoons freshly chopped parsley

320 g (11 oz) Rough Puff Pastry (see page 9) or shop-bought ready-rolled puff pastry

1 beaten egg

salt and pepper

Preheat the oven to 190°C (375°F), gas mark 5.

Make the stuffing as per the instructions on the packet and set aside to cool.

Melt the butter in a large frying pan over a medium heat, add the onion and cook slowly for about 5–10 minutes.

Mix in the flour and then add the stock and the cream. Bring to the boil, then reduce the heat and simmer for 10 minutes. Stir in the chicken, mushrooms and parsley and some salt and pepper. Transfer the mixture to a 1 litre (1¾ pint) pie dish and set aside.

Roll out the pastry on a floured surface so that it is double the size of your pie dish (if you are using ready-rolled you will still need to roll it out to make it big enough).

Get your cooled stuffing and spread a layer of it on top of half the pastry. Fold the other half of the pastry over the top, so that you have a layer of stuffing in the middle. Roll again to press the pastry to the stuffing and to make sure it is large enough to cover your pie dish.

Brush a little of the beaten egg around the rim of the pie dish and then place the pastry over the pie. Fork the edges and skewer 2 little holes in the middle. Brush with beaten egg and cook in the preheated oven for about 35 minutes.

Serve the pie on its own with gravy or, for even more comfort, with some buttery mashed potatoes.

This is a very French tart. The confit garlic goes beautifully with the leeks – it is a little bit of work, but really worth it. It makes a great lunch dish with a fresh green herby salad. Just make sure if you are on a hot date that you both eat it!

Leek & garlic tart

SERVES 4–6

375 g (12 oz) Rough Puff Pastry (see page 9) or shop-bought ready-rolled puff pastry

flour, for dusting

2 garlic bulbs, peeled

2 thyme sprigs

I tablespoon olive oil

200 ml (7 fl oz) water

I tablespoon balsamic vinegar

I teaspoon caster sugar

50 g (2 oz) unsalted butter

12 baby leeks, trimmed

2 eggs

100 ml (3½ fl oz) crème fraîche

100 ml (3½ fl oz) double cream

75 g (3 oz) Gruyère, grated

salt and pepper

Preheat the oven to 180°C (350°F), gas mark 4.

Roll out the pastry on a floured surface to a circle with a diameter of about 30 cm (12 inches). Place in a 25 x 18 cm (10 x 7 inch) tart tin and bake blind in the preheated oven for about 15 minutes. Remove the baking beans, prick the base with a fork and bake for another 5–10 minutes.

Put the garlic cloves and thyme in a saucepan, cover with water and set over a medium heat. Cover and simmer for a few minutes. Drain the water. Put the garlic back in the saucepan, add the olive oil and fry over a high heat for a few minutes.

Add the water and vinegar, bring to the boil and then simmer for about 10 minutes. Add the sugar and some salt and pepper and simmer until the liquid has evaporated – you should be left with the caramelised garlic cloves. Remove the garlic from the pan and set aside.

Melt the butter in the same saucepan over a low heat, add the leeks and some salt and pepper and cook, covered, until they have softened. Spread the leeks on the blind-baked tart case and then top with the garlic.

Mix the eggs, crème fraîche, cream and cheese in a jug or bowl and pour over the garlic and leeks. Turn the oven down to 160°C (325°F), gas mark 3 and bake for 30 minutes until set and golden.

I was lucky enough to go to America for a cooking strand called 'Movie Star Menus' on *This Morning*. I tried and tasted a lot of food and this is just one of the recipes that I came home dreaming about. It is so simple but so refreshing and crunchy and creamy and all the things I want from a salad. What I love about it is that it's exactly what it says – a wedge of iceberg lettuce and blue cheese dressing. I just add a few fresh herbs and some crispy onion rings. All my friends love it.

Iceberg wedge salad with blue cheese dressing

SERVES 4 AS A STARTER

2 small shallots, peeled and finely sliced into rings

vegetable oil, for deep-frying

1 large iceberg lettuce, cut into quarters, the outer leaves removed and the hard inner core cut out

fresh chervil if you can get it or fresh tarragon

FOR THE DRESSING

100 g (3½ oz) soft blue cheese (e.g. Gorgonzola)

250 ml (7 fl oz) double cream

2 tablespoons crème fraîche

juice of 1 lemon

salt and pepper

First, make the dressing. Put nearly all of the cheese (keep a little back to sprinkle over the salad), the cream, crème fraîche, lemon juice, salt and pepper into a food processor and blitz until combined.

For the crispy shallots, drop the shallots into a saucepan and pour over enough oil to cover them. Set over a medium heat and cook gently for 4–5 minutes. As the temperature of the oil increases, the shallots will start to crisp. Once the shallots have turned a deep golden colour, remove from the oil with a slotted spoon and drain on kitchen paper. Sprinkle with a good pinch of salt and set aside.

Place the lettuce on a serving plate and drizzle over the dressing. Scatter the herbs and crispy shallots over the top and finish with the reserved crumbled blue cheese.

The first time I had chicken-fried steak was in a restaurant in LA. Essentially it's a steak dipped in the seasoning for fried chicken – it's very naughty, but very nice.

Chicken-fried steak & creamed corn

SERVES 4

1 garlic clove

2.5 cm (1 inch) piece of fresh ginger

a good pinch of salt

150 ml (¼ pint) condensed cream of chicken soup

150 ml (¼ pint) buttermilk

4 slices of topside steak (tenderised)

2 eggs, beaten with a little salt

400 ml (14 fl oz) vegetable oil

FOR THE COATING

200 g (7 oz) self-raising flour

1 teaspoon salt

1 teaspoon freshly ground black pepper

2 teaspoons cayenne pepper

1 teaspoon dried oregano

1 teaspoon allspice

FOR THE CREAMED CORN

25 g (1 oz) butter

½ onion, finely chopped

1 x 350 g tin sweetcorn, drained

150 ml (¼ pint) double cream

salt and pepper

To make the coating: place all the ingredients in a plastic bag and shake together to mix. Set aside until needed.

Put the garlic, ginger and salt in a pestle and mortar and pound to a paste or use a Magimix. Put in a bowl and add the soup and buttermilk. Mix well. Pour this over the steaks in a shallow dish, making sure they are well coated. Leave for 5 minutes.

Sprinkle the seasoned flour on to a large plate. Take each steak from the marinade and coat both sides of the meat well with seasoned flour. Place them on a wire rack (set over a large plate or the sink) for about 10 minutes until the coating goes soggy.

Meanwhile, make the creamed corn. Melt the butter in a small frying pan over a low heat and slowly cook the onion until softened and just beginning to caramelise. Add the corn and mash it down a little with a potato masher. Add the cream and let the mixture bubble away for 5–10 minutes until the sauce is quite thick. Season to taste and keep warm.

Place the beaten eggs in a shallow dish. Dip each steak in the egg and then again in the seasoned flour, patting down to coat well. Place the steaks on the wire rack and chill for 20 minutes.

Heat half the oil in a deep frying pan over a high heat. Drop in a small cube of bread to check the temperature – it should start to sizzle and brown if the oil is hot enough. When the oil is ready, gently lower half the coated meat into the oil and cook for a good 3 minutes, carefully turn and then cook for another 3 minutes. Use a slotted spoon to lift the steaks out of the oil, place on a clean wire rack (they go soggy on a plate) and keep warm. Add the remaining oil and bring back to the heat. Repeat the process until all of the steaks are cooked. Serve with the corn and a creamy gravy (see page 12), if liked.

My mum used to make chicken Kiev while we were growing up. Yes, you can buy chicken Kiev in every supermarket, but they really are a thousand times more delicious when you make them yourself!

Chicken Kiev

SERVES 4

160 g (5½ oz) butter, softened

2–3 large garlic cloves, finely chopped

4 tablespoons freshly chopped parsley

finely grated zest and juice of 1 lemon

4 free-range skinless chicken breasts

6–8 tablespoons plain flour

1–2 teaspoons paprika

2 large free-range eggs, beaten

200 g (7 oz) dried breadcrumbs

sunflower oil, for frying

salt and pepper

Preheat the oven to 190°C (375°F), gas mark 5.

To make the filling, put the butter with the garlic, parsley, lemon zest, lemon juice, and a pinch of salt and pepper to taste in a bowl and mix together well. Form the garlic butter into 2 logs, using cling film to help you wrap and roll and chill them until firm.

Make a pocket in each chicken breast by cutting a slash lengthways through the breast. Cut the butter logs in half and place one half in each chicken pocket. Secure with cocktail sticks.

Mix the flour, paprika and seasoning together in a shallow bowl. Tip the beaten eggs into another shallow bowl and the breadcrumbs into a third shallow bowl. Toss the stuffed chicken breasts first in the flour to coat, then into the egg and turn until covered. Repeat the flour and egg coating once more. Dip into the breadcrumbs and coat completely.

Pour the oil into a medium frying pan to a depth of about 1 cm (½ inch) and set over a high heat. Check that the oil is hot enough (see page 21) and then lower the chicken breasts carefully into the pan. Spoon hot oil over the top to seal the crumbs for about 1 minute. Turn over to brown the other side, again spooning oil over the top until golden; this should take a further 1–2 minutes.

Remove the chicken from the oil and place in a shallow roasting pan. Bake the chicken in the oven for 10–12 minutes or until the breasts feel firm when pressed. Remove and drain on kitchen paper. Carefully remove the cocktail sticks and serve with mashed potato and green beans.

Roast chicken is the ultimate in comfort food – just walking through the door to the smell of a chicken roasting in the oven is enough to make me breathe a great big sigh. A week before Christmas I was really craving roast chicken, even though I knew I would have my fill of roast dinners over the coming days. I decided to roast the chook and serve it with buttered shallots and thyme and peas. I don't know whether it was just that I was so in the mood for it, or that it really did taste so good, but I felt afterwards that I had given myself the biggest hug in the land!

Perfect roast chicken

SERVES A FAMILY OF 4

1 onion, quartered

1 celery stick, halved

1 carrot, cut into thirds

1 lemon

1 x 1.5 kg (3 lb) chicken

4–5 garlic cloves, skin on but smashed a bit

oil

25 g (1 oz) butter

salt and pepper

FOR THE SHALLOTS

60 g (2¼ oz) butter

8–10 banana shallots, peeled and cut in half at the root

4 thyme sprigs

200 g (7 oz) peas

75–100 ml (3–3½ fl oz) fresh chicken stock

Preheat the oven to 190°C (375°F), gas mark 5.

Place the onion, celery and carrot on a large baking tray. Cut the lemon into wedges and stuff the cavity of the chicken with the garlic and the lemon wedges. Put the chicken on top of the veg and rub the chicken skin with oil. I season it all over and smear the butter over the breasts.

Bake in the preheated oven for 20 minutes per 500 g (1 lb) plus another 20 minutes (usually a 1.5 kg (3 lb) bird takes about 1 hour 20 minutes). Baste every 30 minutes, or about 3 times. Test to see if the chicken is cooked by piercing the flesh at the leg joint with a sharp knife and pressing down gently – if the juices run clear, it should be cooked. Carefully lift the chicken out of the tray and then leave to rest for at least 15 minutes.

While the chicken is resting, prepare the shallots. Melt the butter over a medium-low heat and add the shallots cut side down. Season, add the thyme and let them cook away slowly for a good 10 minutes, turning up the heat a little so that they get a bit of colour.

After 15 minutes, add the peas and a splash of chicken stock and let the pan bubble away for a further 10–15 minutes.

Serve with the roast chicken and some roast potatoes.

I am a massive fan of Gone with the Wind and spent hours at the Margaret Mitchell museum in Atlanta and seeing her house during my time in America. I could envisage Miss Scarlett O'Hara on those tree-lined streets! I found a great Southern food restaurant and had THE most delicious fried chicken, mash and gravy that I have ever tasted.

Southern fried chicken

SERVES 6

I garlic clove

2.5 cm (I inch) piece of fresh ginger

a good pinch of salt

150 ml (¼ pint) condensed cream of chicken soup

150 ml (¼ pint) buttermilk

1.5 kg (3 lb) mixed chicken pieces, skin on, evenly sized and slashed to the bone, soaked in ice-cold water for 20 minutes, drained and patted dry

2 eggs, beaten with a little salt

400 ml (14 fl oz) vegetable oil

Creamy Gravy (see page 12), to serve

lemon or lime wedges, to serve

FOR THE COATING

200 g (7 oz) self-raising flour

I teaspoon salt

I teaspoon ground black pepper

2 teaspoons cayenne pepper

I teaspoon dried oregano

I teaspoon allspice

Preheat the oven to 180°C (350°F), gas mark 4. To make the coating, place the ingredients in a bag, shake and set aside.

Put the garlic, ginger and salt in a pestle and mortar and pound to a paste or use a Magimix. Put in a bowl and add the soup and buttermilk. Mix well. Pour this over the chicken in a shallow dish, making sure it is well coated. Leave for 5 minutes.

Sprinkle the seasoned flour on to a large plate. Take each chicken piece from the marinade and coat well with seasoned flour. Place them on a wire rack (set over a large plate or the sink) for about 10 minutes until the coating goes soggy.

Put the beaten eggs in a shallow dish. Dip each chicken piece in the egg, then in the coating, pressing on both sides again. Place the chicken on the wire rack and chill for 20 minutes.

Position another wire rack in a roasting tin, and put in the preheated oven. Pour the oil into a deep-fryer or heavy-based, straight-sided saucepan and heat to 180°C (350°F). Test to see if the oil is hot enough (see page 21).

Fry in batches, adding the chicken pieces one at a time using tongs. Fry for 8–10 minutes or until each one is golden and crispy. Remove the chicken and drain on crumpled kitchen paper until all the batches are done. Make sure you return the oil to the correct temperature between each addition.

Transfer all the fried chicken to the wire rack in the oven and roast for 20 minutes until cooked (cut open a piece of chicken to check: it should not be pink near the bone). Serve the chicken hot, with the gravy and wedges of lemon or lime.

I used to turn my nose up at the mention of lentils – they conjured up an image of hard orange things that tasted of nothing. However, that was before I tried Puy lentils – and of course tasted them made by people other than my old school dinner ladies. I remember having the most delicious lentil salad in Jamie Oliver's restaurant, Fifteen, and going home and trying to replicate the dish. I wanted to make it a little more substantial and had some beautiful Toulouse casserole sausages that I cooked in a little wine and served with the lentils. It was a really simple dinner and I suddenly felt very French and rustic!

Green lentils with Toulouse sausages

SERVES 4
25 g (1 oz) butter
olive oil, for frying
8 Toulouse sausages
4 shallots, peeled and cut in half lengthways
125 ml (4 fl oz) red wine

FOR THE LENTILS
500 g (1 lb) Puy lentils
1 onion, cut in half at root with 2 cloves stuck in it
1 garlic clove
1 bay leaf
1 teaspoon sugar
50 ml (2 fl oz) red wine vinegar, plus a capful to cook with
25 ml (1 fl oz) olive oil
salt and pepper
fresh crusty bread, to serve

Preheat the oven to 180°C (350°F), gas mark 4.

Heat the butter and a little oil in a large ovenproof frying pan or casserole dish over a medium heat. Add the sausages and shallots and cook until the sausages are browned all over. Add the red wine, cover and put in the preheated oven for 30–40 minutes.

Meanwhile, prepare the lentils. Rinse and drain the lentils and put them in a large lidded saucepan with the onion, garlic and bay leaf. Add enough cold water to cover by about 2.5 cm (1 inch) and add the sugar and capful of vinegar. Put the lid on, set over a medium heat and bring to the boil.

Reduce the heat and simmer on low for about 30 minutes. By the end of the cooking time the water should have been absorbed, but check it throughout the cooking time to ensure the liquid doesn't burn off too quickly – if this is the case, add a little more water. Season to taste.

Whisk the oil and the remaining vinegar together in a small bowl. Drain the lentils and discard the bay leaf, garlic and onion. Pour the oil and vinegar over the lentils and serve with the braised sausages and some crusty bread.

My wonderful friend Dhruv Baker (*MasterChef* winner 2010) and I love cooking together, and do a lot of cooking demos at different food shows. He made this cassoulet at the BBC Good Food Show in Birmingham and in London, while I made the Little Ginger Puddings (see page 46) to serve after. On rehearsal day I was starving and when I get hungry I get moody (Dhruv has nicknamed this The Hanger!). Anyway, as soon as he'd finished cooking this dish, I was there with my fork, and pretty much polished off the whole delicious plate... hunger appeased! I have now well and truly adopted this recipe into my own repertoire. How lucky I am to have MasterChefs as friends!

Cassoulet

SERVES 4

50 ml (2 fl oz) olive oil, plus extra for drizzling

1 carrot, finely chopped

1 onion, peeled and finely chopped

1 celery stick, finely chopped

2 garlic cloves, crushed

4 good-quality Toulouse sausages

2 thyme sprigs

2 bay leaves

2 x 400 g tins chopped tomatoes

1 tablespoon tomato purée

2 x 400 g tins haricot beans

250 ml (8 fl oz) chicken stock

4 confit duck legs (see page 150)

50 g (2 oz) breadcrumbs

2 tablespoons finely chopped fresh parsley

salt and pepper

Heat the olive oil in a large heatproof casserole dish over a medium heat and fry the chopped vegetables until softened and beginning to take on a little colour. Add the garlic and cook for a couple of minutes.

Add the sausages and cook for a few more minutes. Then add the thyme and bay leaves.

Add the tomatoes, tomato purée, beans and stock and cook for a good 10 minutes until the stock has reduced to a lovely thick consistency.

Preheat the grill to medium.

Lay the confit duck legs over the top of the bean and sausage mixture and scatter over the breadcrumbs and the parsley. Drizzle with olive oil, season with salt and pepper and cook under the grill for 10–15 minutes until the breadcrumbs are golden and the duck is warmed through.

This is another of my recipes that I brought home from my trip to America. I had to recreate the jambalaya dish that Pierce Brosnan choked on in the brilliant film, *Mrs Doubtfire*. I had never made a jambalaya before, so spent a Saturday afternoon playing around with it, then took my best version over to Angela's for dinner that night. Every plate was practically licked clean. Their verdict was that it was a winner... so here you go!

Jambalaya

SERVES 4

1–2 tablespoons olive oil

4 chicken breasts, sliced

400 g (13 oz) chorizo, chopped

2 onions, finely sliced

2 garlic cloves, crushed

2 peppers (red, yellow or green), deseeded and sliced

2 celery sticks, chopped

1 teaspoon dried thyme

1 teaspoon dried oregano

¼ teaspoon onion salt

¼ teaspoon garlic salt

1 teaspoon paprika

1 teaspoon cayenne pepper

½ teaspoon mustard powder

a pinch of white pepper

300 g (10 oz) long-grain rice

1 x 400 g tin chopped tomatoes

300 ml (½ pint) chicken stock

300 g (10 oz) prawns

about 12 mussels

about 12 clams

1–2 tablespoons freshly chopped parsley

5 spring onions, sliced

Place a heavy-based casserole dish over a medium-high heat. Add the olive oil and the sliced chicken breasts. When the chicken is starting to brown, add the chorizo and cook for 2–3 minutes until it browns a little too. Use a slotted spoon to remove the chicken and chorizo and set aside on a plate.

Return the pan to the heat and add the onions. Cook until softened and then add the garlic, peppers, celery, thyme and oregano and stir through to mix. Return the chicken and chorizo to the pan, add the onion salt, garlic salt, paprika, cayenne pepper, mustard powder and white pepper. Stir well.

Add the rice, tomatoes and stock and give it a good stir. Bring to the boil and let it simmer, covered, for about 15 minutes or until the rice is cooked through. Give it a good stir every now and then so that it doesn't stick to the base of the pan.

Add the prawns and cook for a few minutes, then add the mussels and clams and cover and cook for about 2–3 minutes or until the shells have opened (discard any that do not open). Sprinkle with the parsley and the spring onions and serve.

I had never made a jambalaya before, so spent a Saturday afternoon playing around with it, then took my best version over to Angela's for dinner. Every plate was practically licked clean!

I remember going into a little pub in London. It was tiny and full of regulars. The menu was only very small and while I was debating what to have, this beautiful pie came out for another of the customers. It smelt and looked amazing; I loved the bone sticking out of the pastry so I promptly ordered it for myself. You know it was good because I've ended up cooking it at home and my version has ended up in my book.

Lamb shank pie

MAKES 1 LARGE PIE

2 lamb shanks

plain flour, for dusting

2 tablespoons olive oil

4 shallots, peeled and quartered lengthways

10–12 Chantenay carrots, washed and halved lengthways

1 garlic clove, finely chopped

150 ml (¼ pint) red wine

1 x 400 g tin chopped tomatoes

1 bay leaf

1 fresh rosemary sprig

1 fresh thyme sprig

1 quantity Rough Puff Pastry (see page 9)

1 egg, beaten

salt and pepper

Preheat the oven to 180°C (350°F), gas mark 4.

Toss the lamb shanks in some seasoned flour. Heat the olive oil in a large frying pan over a medium heat and brown the lamb shanks all over. Set aside in a large enamel pie dish.

Adding more oil if necessary, gently fry the shallots and the carrots for a few minutes and then add the garlic. Cook over a low heat for about 10 minutes. Add the red wine, stirring to incorporate any floury bits stuck to the base of the pan, and bring to the boil. Add the tomatoes and herbs and then spoon into the enamel pie dish over the lamb shanks.

Cover the dish with foil and cook in the preheated oven for about 1¾–2 hours or until the lamb is tender. Once cooked, leave the lamb to cool before covering with pastry.

Preheat the oven to 220°C (425°F), gas mark 7.

Roll out the rough puff pastry to about 5 mm (¼ inch) thick and big enough to cover your pie dish. Carefully place the pastry on top of the cooled lamb shanks in the pie dish, making a cross cut where the bone of the shank sticks up. Gently ease the pastry down around the bone so that it sticks through the pastry lid. Crimp the edges of the pastry and brush with beaten egg to give a nice glaze. Cover the bones with foil when baking the pastry to stop them from burning. Cook in the oven for 20–25 minutes or until golden.

A very dear friend of mine gave me a jar of preserved lemons. They looked so beautiful, but I had never tasted them or used them in cooking before. They have a very strong but delicate flavour and I think they are underused in this country. I was desperate to cook with them, and this is the first dish I made.

Lamb tagine with preserved lemons

SERVES 4–6 DEPENDING ON SIZE OF SHANKS

4–6 lamb shanks

oil, for frying

3 carrots, peeled and cut into quarters

2 red onions, peeled and cut into quarters

a handful of dried apricots

750 ml (1¼ pints) water

2 tablespoons honey

1 tablespoon fish sauce

a squeeze of lemon juice

4–6 slices Preserved Lemons (see page 106), chopped

a handful of mint, chopped

FOR THE PASTE

2 handfuls of flat-leaf parsley

2 handfuls of fresh coriander

½ red onion

6 garlic cloves

5 cm (2 inch) piece of fresh ginger

juice of 1 lemon

150 ml (¼ pint) olive oil

1 tablespoon fish sauce

3 teaspoons paprika

3 teaspoons ground cumin

3 teaspoons turmeric

2 teaspoons chilli powder

To make the paste, put all the ingredients in a food processor or blender and blitz.

Stab the lamb shanks with a sharp knife a few times – this is to help infuse the flavours and the meat to easily fall off the bone. Cover the shanks in the paste and leave to marinate for at least 3 hours, but preferably overnight.

Preheat the oven to 200°C (400°F), gas mark 6.

Heat a little oil in a large casserole, tagine dish or baking tray. Add the marinated shanks and cook until they are beginning to brown all over. Add the carrots, onions and apricots. Pour over the water and then cover the dish with greaseproof paper and then foil.

Put the dish in the preheated oven for 5–10 minutes, then turn the oven down to 160°C (325°F), gas mark 3 and cook for 3–4 hours.

Remove the dish from the oven and season with the honey, the fish sauce and a squeeze of lemon juice. Stir through the preserved lemons and fresh mint.

Serve with couscous and harissa if liked.

I love roast beef and Yorkshire pudding! Sunday to me is not Sunday without roast dinner. I actually think that making a roast is one of the nicest things to do, as long as you give yourself the time to do it. The meat needs to come out of the fridge at least 30 minutes before you cook it, and allow plenty of resting time. This also gives you more oven space, for your Yorkshires and your roasties. I always think a rib of beef is the tastiest – it also looks so lovely when you bring it to the table.

Roast rib of beef

SERVES 4—6

3-bone rib of beef

oil, for rubbing

1 teaspoon mustard powder

salt and pepper

FOR THE YORKSHIRE PUDDINGS

250 g (9 oz) plain flour

2 eggs

500 ml (17 fl oz) milk

Note: Just remember that all ovens are different and every piece of meat is different, so time schedules can vary.

Variation: To pep up your Yorkshires, you could also add 1 teaspoon horseradish or mustard powder.

Preheat the oven to 230°C (450°F), gas mark 8. Rub the beef joint with oil, score the fat and then season with a little salt and pepper and sprinkle with mustard powder.

Put the beef on a large baking tray and cook in the oven for about 20 minutes. Turn the heat down to 190°C (375°F), gas mark 5 and cook for a further 15 minutes per 500 g (1 lb) for rare; 20 minutes per 500 g (1 lb) for medium; and 30 minutes per 500 g (1 lb) for well done. I like to baste the meat about 3–4 times during cooking.

Meanwhile, prepare the Yorkshires. Sift the flour into a large bowl and make a well in the centre. In a jug, beat together the eggs, milk and a pinch of salt, then pour into the well and whisk until smooth. Add some black pepper and mix again.

About 5–10 minutes before you take your meat out of the oven, drain off some of the beef fat and pour into a baking tray with a little extra oil if needed and place over a medium heat on the hob.

When the beef is cooked, remove it from the oven and leave the meat to rest for at least 30 minutes. Keep the oven temperature the same.

Pour your batter into the hot oil in the baking tray and cook in the oven for about 25 minutes.

Carve and serve the beef with the Yorkshires and any other additions you desire for your perfect roast dinner.

What's great about this dish is that, as well as being quick, it is also the ultimate comfort food and a little different from steak and mash! I can't stand bland polenta, so I like lots of butter, pepper and Parmesan in mine.

Steak with polenta & caramelised onions

SERVES 4

olive oil, for frying

25 g (1 oz) unsalted butter, plus a little extra for frying

3 large onions, finely sliced

2 thyme sprigs

2 teaspoons brown sugar

1 tablespoon sherry vinegar

4 rib-eye or sirloin steaks, each around 175–200 g (6–7 oz)

100 ml (3½ fl oz) Madeira

300 ml (¼ pint) dark beef stock

a large knob of cold unsalted butter

sea salt and pepper

green vegetables, to serve

FOR THE POLENTA

600 ml (1 pint) chicken or vegetable stock

150 g (5 oz) quick-cook polenta

25 g (1 oz) unsalted butter

50 g (2 oz) Parmesan cheese, finely grated

Heat a little oil in a heavy-based frying pan over a low heat, add the butter and, when foaming, add the onions and thyme. Cook gently for 20–25 minutes until caramelised. Add the sugar and vinegar and cook for a further 10 minutes until dark and sticky. Keep warm until serving.

Meanwhile, heat a large heavy-based frying pan over a high heat until smoking. Rub the steaks with a little oil and season with salt and pepper. Sear for 3–4 minutes on each side, depending on how you like your steak to be cooked. Transfer the steaks to a warm plate and leave to rest for 10 minutes.

Return the steak pan to the heat and deglaze with the Madeira. Pour in the beef stock and boil until reduced by two-thirds. Pour in any resting juices from the steaks and then remove the pan from the heat and whisk in a knob of cold butter. Season to taste.

For the polenta, bring the stock to the boil in a large saucepan over a medium heat and then quickly whisk in the polenta (make sure you whisk continuously to prevent it from turning lumpy). Turn down the heat and keep whisking for 2 minutes or until the polenta has thickened and starts to pull away from the sides of the pan. Remove from the heat, whisk in the butter and Parmesan and season.

To serve, place a large spoonful of polenta in the middle of a warm serving plate. Lay the steaks on top of the polenta and serve with the caramelised onions, a drizzle of gravy and some simple green vegetables.

Another American classic – I told you I had fallen in love with that vast country. I sat eating these in a little roadside diner on my way to Dollywood (I love Dolly Parton and her theme park is ace!). Frickles (fried pickles) are inspired and served with a blue cheese dipping sauce (see page 20). The ribs are messy, gooey, sticky – and they leave you with a massive grin on your face!

Short ribs & frickles

SERVES 4–6

1 kg (2 lb) beef short ribs, cut into 7.5 cm (3 inch) lengths

I large onion, chopped

1 x 400 g tin chopped tomatoes

3 tablespoons tomato ketchup

½–1 jalapeño chilli, deseeded and finely chopped

3 tablespoons red wine vinegar

3 tablespoons demerara sugar

1 green pepper, deseeded and finely chopped

1½ teaspoons mustard powder

4 garlic cloves, finely chopped

¼ teaspoon chilli powder (or more to taste)

a pinch of ground cloves

a pinch of ground cinnamon

250 ml (9 fl oz) sweet dark beer, such as Newcastle Brown

a handful of coriander, chopped

FOR THE FRICKLES

100 g (3½ oz) self-raising flour

100 g (3½ oz) cornflour

250 ml (9 fl oz) iced sparkling water

vegetable oil, for frying

6–8 large gherkins, sliced

Preheat the oven to 150°C (300°F), gas mark 2. Arrange the short ribs in a single layer in a large roasting tray. Sprinkle the onion around the ribs.

Put all the remaining ingredients, except the beer and coriander, in a large saucepan and simmer over a medium heat for about 10 minutes until slightly thickened.

Leave to cool slightly and then stir in the beer. Pour the mixture over the ribs, cover the baking pan tightly with foil and bake in the preheated oven for 2½–3 hours, or until the ribs are very tender.

Meanwhile, make the frickles. Sift the flour and cornflour together into a bowl. Mix in enough iced water to make a batter that will coat the back of a spoon. Heat a pan of oil for deep-frying over a medium heat until it reaches a temperature of about 180°C (350°F). Test to see if the oil is hot enough (see page 21).

Dip the gherkin slices into the batter before deep-frying in batches for a couple of minutes until golden and crispy. Drain on kitchen paper.

When the ribs are cooked, remove them from the pan and keep warm. Skim off the fat from the roasting tray and pour the remaining sauce into a clean saucepan. Boil over a medium heat until reduced and thickened slightly. Pour the sauce over the ribs, sprinkle with coriander and serve with the deep-fried frickles.

This is one of John Torode's recipes. He makes the best Thai curry in the land!

Thai curry

SERVES 6—8

FOR THE CURRY PASTE

1 tablespoon coriander stalks

1 teaspoon coriander seeds

1 teaspoon ground cumin

15 g (¾ oz) white pepper

6 large green chillies

2 small green chillies

2 lemongrass stalks

2 Thai shallots, chopped

2 garlic cloves, peeled

1 thumb-size piece of galangal

grated zest of 1 lime

10 g (½ oz) shrimp paste

1 teaspoon salt

2 handfuls of Thai basil

2 handfuls of coriander

FOR THE CURRY

300 g (10 oz) sweet potato

6 Thai aubergines

3 long green chillies

500 g (1 lb) chicken thigh fillet

300 ml (½ pint) thick coconut milk

2 tablespoons palm sugar

1 dessertspoon fish sauce

300 ml (½ pint) thin coconut milk

200 g (7 oz) fresh prawns

100 g (3½ oz) green beans

6 lime leaves, torn

salt and pepper

To make the paste, toast all the spices in a hot frying pan until fragrant, and then grind to a powder in a mortar and pestle.

Chop the chillies, then strip the lemongrass stalks and chop roughly. Put them in a food processor and add the remaining ingredients, except the toasted spice powder. Blend until smooth (you may need to add a little water). Add the spice powder, blend again until smooth and set aside.

To make the curry, first prepare the vegetables and meat. Peel the sweet potatoes and cut into cubes, and split the aubergines in half. Julienne the long green chillies and then cut the chicken into small pieces.

Heat the thick coconut milk in a saucepan over a medium heat until the milk splits and bubbles and splutters. Add 4 tablespoons of the green curry paste (freeze any leftover paste) and fry, stirring, for 3 minutes until fragrant.

Add the palm sugar and fish sauce, cook for 2 minutes and then add the sweet potato and aubergines. Fry in the paste for a good 2 minutes. Add the thin coconut milk and bring to the boil. Cook for 10 minutes and then add the chicken and cook for a further 5 minutes, boiling really vigorously. Add the prawns, green beans, lime leaves and julienned green chillies and heat through for a few minutes. Turn off the heat, then taste and season.

Serve with Thai jasmine fragrant rice.

Note: Thick coconut milk is the thicker liquid in a tin of coconut milk that hasn't been shaken to mix and thin coconut milk is the liquid underneath.

In my last book, I included my mum's tried and tested pavlova recipe. Lots of people really loved it – I wanted to create a variation on the same theme, and seeing as I have a (little!) bit of an obsession with chocolate this is what I came up with. It's a great 'occasion' pud because you could decorate with chocolate coins at Christmas or mini eggs at Easter… or I think malted chocolate balls would be delicious… you get the picture!

Chocolate pavlova

SERVES 4–6

4 egg whites

a pinch of salt

200 g (7 oz) caster sugar

2 tablespoons cocoa powder, sifted

1 teaspoon vanilla extract

1 teaspoon malt vinegar

200 g (7 oz) dark chocolate, chopped

400 ml (14 fl oz) double cream

Preheat the oven to 140°C (275°F), gas mark 1. Draw a 23 cm (9 inch) circle on non-stick paper as a guide and place on a flat baking tray.

Whisk the egg whites with the salt in a large clean bowl, either by hand or with a hand-held electric mixer, until very stiff and then gradually whisk in the sugar. Whisk until it forms stiff peaks – this takes about 3–4 minutes. Gradually fold in the cocoa powder, then the vanilla extract and the vinegar.

Spread the meringue mixture over the circle on the non-stick paper and bake in the preheated oven for 1 hour, until firm. Turn off the oven and leave the meringue in for another 30 minutes with the door closed. Leave the meringue to cool and then very carefully peel off the baking paper from the bottom. Place the pavlova on a serving plate.

Meanwhile, put the chocolate and 100 ml (3½ fl oz) of the double cream in a heatproof bowl and place over a pan of simmering water (making sure the bowl doesn't touch the water). Melt the chocolate and cream together, stirring until smooth. Leave to cool down to room temperature.

Whip the remaining cream and spoon over the meringue. Drizzle the chocolate sauce over the top and then use a skewer or the handle of a teaspoon to swirl and marble the chocolate through the cream.

I first made these puddings for a demo at one of the BBC Good Food Shows. My wonderful friend Dhruv Baker (*MasterChef* winner 2010) and I did a lot of demos together and had a lot of fun. His food is delicious; he had made the Cassoulet (see page 28) and I made these puddings. Very easy and very light, and the cardamom crème anglaise is so subtle but really works.

Little ginger puddings with cardamom crème anglaise

SERVES 8

FOR THE PUDDINGS

75 g (3 oz) butter, plus extra for greasing

icing sugar and ground ginger, mixed, for dusting

2 tablespoons black treacle

150 ml (¼ pint) warm water

175 g (6 oz) self-raising flour

100 g (3½ oz) Muscovado sugar

2.5 cm (1 inch) piece of fresh ginger, grated

¼ teaspoon ground ginger

1 teaspoon allspice

½ teaspoon baking powder

¾ teaspoon bicarbonate of soda

2 eggs

6 pieces of stem ginger, finely chopped

FOR THE CARDAMOM CRÈME ANGLAISE

250 ml (9 fl oz) milk

250 ml (9 fl oz) double cream

6 cardamom pods, bashed

6 egg yolks

65 g (2½ oz) caster sugar

Preheat the oven to 180°C (350°F), gas mark 4. Grease 8 dariole moulds and dust them with a mix of icing sugar and ground ginger. Melt the butter and treacle in a saucepan over a medium heat until simmering, then add the warm water.

Sift the flour into a large bowl and then add the sugar, fresh ginger, ground ginger, allspice, baking powder and bicarbonate of soda and mix thoroughly. Add the eggs and the melted treacle butter and mix together with a hand-held electric whisk. Fold in the finely chopped stem ginger.

Pour the mixture into the prepared moulds, no more than two-thirds full. Place on a baking tray in the preheated oven and cook for about 13–15 minutes.

Meanwhile, make the crème anglaise: heat the milk, cream and cardamom pods in a heavy-based saucepan over a very low heat until simmering. Remove from the heat and pour into a jug (this ensures the milk is not too hot).

Whisk the egg yolks and sugar in a bowl until almost white in colour. Pour a little of the milk on to the eggs, mix and then add the rest. Return to the pan and stir continuously until the mixture coats the back of a spoon. Pour the crème anglaise through a fine sieve and discard the cardamoms.

Take the puddings out of the oven. They will have risen, so level out the tops with a knife and then turn out and serve with the crème anglaise.

The Good Food Shows have become part of my life. Hanging out with like-minded super-obsessed foodies! The *MasterChef* lot are a huge part of that. One man in particular is my friend John Gilbert, who is basically my 'show husband'. We got talking recently about cheesecakes; I said I wasn't keen on baked ones; he said that his recipe would change that. It has made its way into my book, so I must be converted!

John Gilbert's cheesecake

SERVES 4—6

125 g (4 oz) unsalted butter, very soft, plus extra for greasing

375 g (9 oz) digestive biscuits, crushed

600 g (1 lb 2 oz) cream cheese

200 g (7 oz) sugar

1½ tablespoons good-quality vanilla extract

3 eggs

275 ml (9 fl oz) soured cream

Preheat the oven to 180°C (350°F), gas mark 4. Grease a 20-cm (8-inch) springform cake tin with a little butter.

Place the digestive crumbs in a bowl, add the butter and mix thoroughly with your fingers until well combined. Put the moist crumbs into the prepared cake tin and press them firmly down on to the base and up as far on the sides as you can get (don't worry if this looks a bit messy and uneven).

Place the cream cheese in a big clean bowl and beat, either by hand or with a hand-held electric mixer, until a little fluffy, about 2 minutes. Using a spatula, bring the fluffy cream cheese back together. Add the sugar and the vanilla, beat for 1 minute and then spatula the mix together again.

Beat in the eggs, one at a time, and then the soured cream. Scrape down the sides to make sure the whole mixture is blended together. Give it a quick beat so that you are left with a smooth mixture and pour into the cake tin.

Place the tin in the preheated oven and bake for 50 minutes until the cheesecake has risen a bit and is spotted brown in places (it may even have a small crack or two – that's all perfectly fine).

Take the tin out of the oven and leave to cool for 1–2 hours. Once cool, take the cheesecake out of the springform tin, put it in an airtight container and transfer to the fridge. It needs to be in the fridge for at least 4 hours (preferably overnight), and it's still great for a couple of days after that.

We have spent the past few New Years out in a beautiful gîte in Normandy. Unfortunately Sarah, the owner, is selling it, but we will keep such lovely memories of our times there, most of them having something to do with food. Sarah makes the most delicious pear tarte tatin – the first year we tried it we all took the recipe home and made it religiously for about six months, so I had to include it in this chapter. The pastry is flaky, not puff, and the trick is to just combine it and then leave it. I have also made this tart with apples and using shop-bought puff pastry and it works just as well, but the flaky pastry has the edge... go on, give it a go!

Pear tarte tatin

SERVES 6

100 g (3½ oz) unsalted butter

about 8 pears, peeled, cored and cut into quarters lengthways

100 g (3½ oz) caster sugar

1 vanilla pod

1 quantity chilled Flaky Pastry (see page 8)

ice cream or crème fraîche, to serve

Preheat the oven to 220°C (425°F), gas mark 7.

Melt the butter in a heavy-based frying pan over a medium heat and add the pears and the sugar. Split open the vanilla pod, scrape the seeds into the pan and drop in the empty pod. Stir so that the pears don't stick. Cook for about 20 minutes, then turn the heat up and cook for a further 10–15 minutes. You want the pears and sugary butter to go a lovely golden brown, all sticky and caramelised, but not burnt, so keep watching them and shake the pan to stop them from sticking. Pour the pears and juices into a 25 cm (10 inch) pie dish, discarding the vanilla pod (or leave in the pan if it is ovenproof).

Roll out your chilled pastry on a floured surface to slightly larger than the pie dish. I keep it between the greaseproof paper and roll it out that way, to about 1 cm (½ inch) thick. Lay the pastry over the pears and tuck it in around the edges to form an upside-down tart. Bake in the preheated oven for about 30–40 minutes. Leave to cool.

When cooled, place a large serving dish over the top of the pie dish or frying pan and carefully turn it over. Serve warm or at room temperature with ice cream or crème fraîche.

I think this may be my new favourite pudding to make – perfect after a Sunday roast with a house full of people. I never used to like puddings but over the last few years I realise I am developing a sweet tooth and this tart with custard and raspberries really hits the spot! Be sure to give the raspberries their full soaking time, for both texture and flavour.

Raspberry custard tart

SERVES 4—6

50 g (2 oz) caster sugar

100 ml (3½ fl oz) Framboise or similar liqueur

250 g (9 oz) fresh raspberries

I quantity Sweet Pastry (see page 214)

flour, for dusting

butter, for greasing

I egg, beaten

FOR THE CUSTARD

900 ml (1½ pints) double cream

3 eggs

175 g (6 oz) vanilla sugar (see Note below)

75 g (3 oz) unsalted butter, diced

4 tablespoons Framboise or similar liqueur

Note: To make vanilla sugar, fill a jar with caster sugar and push in 1–2 split vanilla pods. Seal and leave to infuse until needed. You can also buy this ready-made.

Mix the sugar with the Framboise in a bowl and then add the raspberries. Leave to soak for about 20 minutes.

Preheat the oven to 180°C (350°F), gas mark 4.

Roll out the pastry on a lightly floured surface into a round about 5 mm (⅛ inch) thick and use it to line a 23 cm (9 inch) greased loose-bottomed flan tin. Transfer to the fridge to chill for 30 minutes, then line with greaseproof paper, fill with baking beans, and bake blind for 15 minutes.

Remove the beans and paper, brush with the beaten egg and bake for a further 5 minutes, or until the pastry is dry and just beginning to colour. Leave the tin on a wire rack to cool. Keep the oven at the same temperature.

Scatter the soaked berries into the blind-baked tart shell.

To make the custard, mix the cream, eggs, vanilla sugar, butter and Framboise together in a bowl, and pour on top of the raspberries. Bake the tart in the preheated oven for 35–40 minutes or until just cooked (the centre should still be slightly soft). Leave the tart to cool on a wire rack for at least 30 minutes, to allow it to set before removing from the tin. Once cool, cut the tart into large wedges and serve.

THE WAY I COOK...

on a Sunday Morning

I'm not a fan of Sundays, I never have been, but Sunday mornings are the best part of the day for me, because you have a licence to be lazy, to actually enjoy breakfast, to take time over it; to think, 'Mmm, I really fancy something different from my everyday cereal or toast.' I want people to read this chapter and be inspired to make Oeufs en Cocotte (see page 66) or Cowboy Breakfast (see page 60), to be able to sit and read the papers or mooch about and, if anyone else is like me... maybe enjoy Sundays just that little bit more!

For the past three years I have been lucky enough to be involved in a Canadian TV series called *The Murdoch Mysteries*. Each summer I have skipped off to Toronto to film this Victorian period drama, and I have met some of the nicest people, actors and crew alike. However, my biggest ally, and now great friend, is the make-up lady, Deb. She is a truly inspirational woman, with her own fabulous make-up range, and a writer too. But I digress... Deb is a proper foodie and we spend hours in the make-up bus comparing recipes and talking food – a few recipes in this book started from conversations with Deb, and this is her French toast muffin recipe, which I think is a great breakfast treat. The muffins freeze well too.

French toast muffins

MAKES 12 MUFFINS

3 eggs

375 ml (13 fl oz) milk

75 g (3 oz) caster sugar

3 teaspoons vanilla extract

100 g (3½ oz) self-raising flour

1 teaspoon ground cinnamon

10 brown or white bread slices

200 g (7 oz) frozen berries

2 tablespoons maple syrup

Note: As a recipe for French toast this naturally contains cinnamon. Anyone who knows me will realise that I'm not a lover of it, and I always take it out of recipes – but to stay true to Deb it's in here!

Preheat the oven to 190°C (375°F), gas mark 5 and line a 12-hole muffin tin with paper cases.

Whisk together the eggs, milk, sugar, vanilla, flour and cinnamon in a bowl.

Cut the bread into cubes and add to the mixture, then stir in the fruit. Divide evenly into the greased muffin tins.

Bake in the preheated oven for 25 minutes until golden. Leave to cool on a wire rack.

The first time I made these I couldn't quite believe how easy they were (granted, I do have my beloved Magimix) and also just how much they looked like the ones I used to buy every week. I have to tell you that one of my guilty pleasures is a well-known fast-food chain's egg and bacon breakfast muffin (I know!), but now I can make my very own version, and it tastes even nicer. They also freeze beautifully.

English muffins

MAKES 8 MUFFINS

25 g (1 oz) unsalted butter

2 teaspoons caster sugar

300 ml (½ pint) whole milk

1 x 7 g sachet dried yeast

450 g (14½ oz) strong white flour

a pinch of sea salt

50 g (2 oz) dry polenta

Put the butter and sugar in a small saucepan and heat gently until the butter has melted. Remove from the heat and pour in the milk. Whisk in the yeast and set aside.

Pour the flour and salt into the bowl of an electric mixer fitted with a dough hook and set the machine on its second lowest setting. Gradually pour in the milk and yeast mixture until fully combined and knead the mixture for 10 minutes.

Turn the dough out into a large clean bowl, cover with cling film and leave to rise in a warm place for 30 minutes.

Sprinkle the work surface with half of the polenta and turn out the dough. Using your hands, gently flatten the dough into a large rectangle, roughly 1.5 cm (¾ inch) thick, and dust the top with the remaining polenta. Use an 8 cm (3¼ inch) round cutter to cut out 8 circles of dough, re-rolling the scraps if needed. Space the muffins out evenly on a large non-stick baking tray and leave to rise for 20 minutes.

Heat a large frying pan over a medium-high heat and cook the muffins (you may need to cook in batches) for 10–12 minutes, turning occasionally, until risen and golden brown.

Serve warm, cut in half and spread with butter. If you leave them to cool, cut them in half and toast until golden before spreading with butter or topping with a poached egg and hollandaise sauce or with bacon, cheese and a fried egg.

Every weekend Billie asks me if we can make pancakes. I always want savoury and B always wants sweet. Usually I make these three variations: bacon to make me happy; blueberries for Billie; and peanut butter and banana for all of us. I also love making these plain and serving them with really crispy streaky bacon and drizzles of maple syrup. American breakfasts are my favourite!

American pancakes

MAKES ABOUT 12 PANCAKES

350 ml (12 fl oz) milk

2 eggs

200 g (7 oz) plain flour

2 teaspoons baking powder

I teaspoon caster sugar

a pinch of salt

If you have a blender, pour in the milk and eggs and blend, then add the flour, baking powder, sugar and salt and blend again. If not, sift the flour and baking powder into a large bowl, add the salt and sugar, and combine. Make a well in the centre, whisk the milk and eggs together in a jug and pour into the well and beat together.

Place a non-stick frying pan over a medium-high heat and brush with a little vegetable oil. When the pan is hot, pour in just over half a ladleful of the batter so that it makes a pancake about 10 cm (4 inches) in diameter. Once bubbles start forming, the pancake is ready to turn over.

Once you've turned the pancake, cook for 30 seconds or so, until golden.

TOPPINGS:

... with pancetta and maple syrup: Follow the method above but also fry 75 g (3 oz) cubed pancetta in a non-stick frying pan. Sprinkle some of the pancetta on each pancake once you've flipped it and then serve with a drizzle of maple syrup.

... with peanut butter and banana: Make the basic batter and add 2–4 tablespoons crunchy peanut butter. Follow the method above, except before you turn the pancakes, add a few slices of banana and cook until golden.

... with blueberries: Make the basic pancake batter and follow the method for cooking, but add a sprinkling of blueberries just before you turn each pancake and then cook until golden.

This is a delicious brunch sandwich and the green tomatoes are a lovely addition; however, if you can't get them just use humble red ones.

BLFGT (bacon, lettuce & fried green tomatoes)

SERVES 4

olive oil, for frying

12 smoked streaky bacon rashers

50 g (2 oz) plain flour

2 eggs, beaten

50 g (2 oz) dry polenta

4 green tomatoes, thickly sliced

8 white farmhouse bread slices

good-quality mayonnaise

2 baby gem lettuces, leaves separated

salt and pepper

Heat a little oil in a frying pan, add the bacon and fry for 4–5 minutes until golden and crisp. Remove from the pan and drain on kitchen paper.

Season the flour with salt and pepper in a shallow bowl and put the beaten eggs and polenta in two other separate shallow bowls. Add the tomato slices to the flour and toss to coat. Dip the slices in the beaten egg and then in the polenta, making sure the slices are evenly coated.

Add a little more oil to the bacon pan and fry the tomato slices in batches for 2 minutes on each side until crisp and golden. Remove from the pan and drain on kitchen paper.

Spread the slices of bread with mayonnaise and give them a good grind of black pepper. Now assemble your sandwich – place 3 bacon slices on top of the mayonnaise, add some slices of fried green tomatoes and a few lettuce leaves and top with another slice of bread. Repeat for the other sandwiches.

I love this breakfast – my best friend Nicola came back from her cousins' one weekend full of excitement at what food she'd eaten, the cowboy breakfast being the highlight! I love the fact that everything just goes in the oven, though how cowboys had ovens I'm not sure. I think it's probably just the fact that everything goes in the same pan. Easy peasy.

Cowboy breakfast

SERVES 4

2 tablespoons olive oil

1 large potato, cut into wedges

8 chipolata sausages

8 streaky bacon rashers

4 plum tomatoes, halved

4 eggs

salt

Preheat the oven to 190°C (375°F), gas mark 5.

Pour the oil into a large shallow ovenproof dish or pan with a metal handle and heat for a few minutes over a medium heat. Add the potato wedges, coat with the hot oil and a little salt, and then transfer the pan to the preheated oven and bake for 10 minutes.

After 10 minutes, turn the potatoes and then add the sausages and bacon. Return to the oven for 20 minutes.

Add the tomatoes and crack the eggs over the top of everything. Cook for a further 5–6 minutes or until the egg whites have set.

Serve with toast and a big pot of tea.

This makes a great brunch for when friends are over and the sun is shining.

Sweetcorn fritters with chorizo salsa & soured cream

SERVES 4

100 g (3½ oz) plain flour

1 teaspoon baking powder

1 egg

125 ml (4 fl oz) milk

300 g (10 oz) sweetcorn

1–2 tablespoons oil

salt and pepper

soured cream, to serve

FOR THE SALSA

2 tablespoons olive oil

1 red onion, finely chopped

150 g (5 oz) chorizo, chopped

1 garlic clove, finely chopped

400 g (13 oz) fresh tomatoes, chopped

1 tablespoon tomato purée

1 teaspoon caster sugar

2 tablespoons finely chopped coriander, plus extra to garnish

Sift the flour, baking powder and some salt into a bowl. Make a well in the centre.

In a jug, beat together the egg and milk and pour into the flour. Whisk until you have a reasonably thick batter (you may not need to use all the milk).

Put the sweetcorn in another bowl and add the batter. You may not need to use all the batter – you are aiming for quite a thick sweetcorn mixture.

Heat the oil in a frying pan over a medium heat and, when hot, spoon in tablespoons of the batter. Fry for a few minutes on each side. Keep warm while you make the salsa.

Heat the oil in a frying pan, add the onion and cook over a medium heat until soft. Add the chorizo and the garlic, and, once the chorizo has a nice bit of colour, add the tomatoes and the purée. Season and cook until the tomatoes have softened and the sauce is coming together but still chunky. Stir in the sugar and cook for a further minute. Stir through the coriander.

Serve the salsa warm, on top of the fritters, with a dollop of soured cream and an extra sprinkle of coriander.

One of the films we looked at for my 'Movie Star Menus' cooking strand filmed for *This Morning* was *When Harry Met Sally*. We went to Katz's deli, the setting for the notorious 'I'll have what she's having' scene. I was so excited to go – they even have a table there with a sign over it saying: 'Where Harry met Sally... hope you have what she had! Enjoy!' I met the chef there and he taught me how to make latkes (similar to a potato rosti). They were so delicious and so reminiscent of this iconic Jewish deli that I had to include them.

Potato latkes

SERVES 4–6

2 large potatoes

¼ onion, grated

1 egg, beaten

1½ tablespoons plain flour

oil, for frying

salt and pepper

Grate the potatoes on to some kitchen paper or a tea towel and squeeze out the excess moisture.

Add the onion to the potato in a bowl. Mix in the beaten egg, some salt and pepper, and then mix in the flour.

Set a frying pan over a medium heat and add the oil. Drop dessertspoonfuls of potato mixture into the hot pan and cook until golden brown. Turn the latkes over and brown the other side. Drain on kitchen paper.

Serve the latkes with soured cream and apple sauce, in true deli style, or with smoked salmon and a wedge of lemon.

The very name of these makes me want to eat them! Little ramekin dishes with an egg, cream, a little spinach and/or pancetta or a drizzle of truffle oil, salt and pepper baked in the oven. Old-fashioned tea or, in my case, brunch at its very best.

Oeufs en cocotte

SERVES 4

50 g (2 oz) butter

200 g (7 oz) spinach

4 pancetta slices

4 eggs

4 tablespoons double cream

truffle oil, for drizzling
(optional)

salt and pepper

sourdough toast, to serve

Preheat the oven to 180°C (350°F), gas mark 4.

Melt the butter in a frying pan over a medium heat and then add the spinach with a little salt and pepper and cook until it is just wilted. Set aside.

If the pancetta is not cooked, put it in the hot frying pan and brown. Set aside.

Arrange a little of the wilted spinach in the base of 4 ramekin dishes and top with the pancetta slices. Make a little well in the middle. Crack an egg into the well in each dish and pour a tablespoon of cream on top, keeping the yolk clear. Add a little drizzle of truffle oil, if you are using.

Add a good grind of salt and pepper and put the ramekin dishes on a baking tray filled with enough warm water to come just about halfway up the dishes.

Bake in the oven for about 6–8 minutes or until the egg whites are just set. Serve with sourdough toast soldiers.

Everybody has their preferred way of cooking eggs. I am (as a lot of people will tell you) quite high maintenance in the egg department, and so these are my tips for getting them just so.

Perfect eggs – my way!

BOILED This is my favourite way to have an egg. My grandma used to peel them soft-boiled and boiling hot and serve with bacon, but I also love them in an egg cup with soldiers. The yolk HAS to be runny but the white HAS to be cooked! Nothing worse than a runny white… well, a few things…

Place 1 egg (Clarence Court Burford Browns if possible) in a saucepan of boiling water (nicely boiling, not angrily!) for 5 minutes. Once done, put the egg in a bowl of really cold water to stop the egg cooking and then take out and put it in your egg cup with some delicious white toast buttered soldiers and some salt and pepper… the breakfast of champions!

FRIED So with a fried egg, if I'm going to eat the white it has to have those lovely salty, buttery crispy edges and again a runny yolk… Heat a frying pan, add a good-sized knob of butter and melt. Add your egg and teaspoon the melted butter over the top of the egg as it starts to set. Keep spooning the butter over the yolk – it will go slightly nutty and be delicious. Cook until you like the look of the yolk, but I do mine for about a minute.

POACHED I use a medium saucepan and fill with just about 2.5 cm (1 inch) of water. When it comes to a rolling boil, add a capful of white wine vinegar. Crack your egg into a small cup or bowl and then pour into the saucepan. Cook for about 2–3 minutes.

If you want to have these prepared in advance, place the poached eggs into a bowl of iced water, and then place on a plate or small baking tray. When you need them, place the eggs into a pan of boiling water on a slotted spoon for about 30 seconds to reheat.

Note: I had the most amazing poached eggs on toasted rye bread with avocado and lemon juice – sounds strange but tasted beautiful!

SCRAMBLED I usually work on the basis of 2 eggs per person and then I add an extra one for luck!

So, to serve 4, I would use 9 eggs, 50 g (2 oz) butter, a dash of cream if I have any in the fridge and some salt and pepper.

Beat all the ingredients together in a bowl. Add to a non-stick saucepan over a medium heat. Keep stirring until the eggs are just cooked but still a little runny. Take off the heat so the heat of the pan will cook the eggs through without making them rubbery. Serve with a good grind of black pepper and an English Muffin (see page 57) or bagel.

There is a little farm café up the road from my house, and they do a great weekend breakfast. My favourite thing to have there is the mushrooms on toast. It's funny, there are no airs and graces at this café and not a herb in sight, but the breakfasts taste home-cooked, and it feels just like I've pitched up at my grandma's house circa 1982!

Mushrooms on toast

SERVES 4

4 white farmhouse bread slices

50 g (2 oz) butter

350 g (11½ oz) field mushrooms, sliced

1 fresh thyme sprig

2 tablespoons crème fraîche

salt and pepper

Toast the bread lightly on both sides and keep warm.

Melt the butter in a frying pan over a medium heat, add the mushrooms and thyme and cook until soft.

Add the crème fraîche and mix together. Season with a good sprinkling of salt and a good grind of black pepper. Discard the thyme sprig.

Spoon the mushrooms on to the toast and serve immediately.

I first had these in LA and it was love at first bite! Eggs, tortillas and spicy tomato sauce... yum.

Huevos rancheros

SERVES 4

4 corn tortillas or other flatbreads

oil, for frying

4 large eggs

freshly chopped coriander, to garnish

FOR THE TOMATO SAUCE

2 tablespoons olive oil

1 large onion, finely chopped

1–2 red chillies, deseeded and finely chopped

2 garlic cloves, finely chopped

2 x 400 g tins plum tomatoes

1 teaspoon brown sugar

salt and pepper

First, make the tomato sauce. Heat the oil in a wide saucepan and soften the onion and the chilli over a low heat for about 10 minutes or until soft.

Add the garlic and continue to cook for 4 minutes. Add the tomatoes, breaking them up a bit when stirring them in, and then add the sugar. Leave to cook for 15–20 minutes until the tomatoes have cooked down and the sauce has thickened. You can add a bit of water if it gets too thick. Season with some salt and pepper.

Dry fry the tortillas in a frying pan or you could brush them with oil and bake them in the oven until crispy. Fry the eggs in the frying pan.

To assemble the breakfast, top each tortilla with a couple of spoonfuls of the tomato sauce and then a fried egg (and any other toppings you would like, see below). Garnish with coriander.

VARIATIONS:

You can add grated cheese, sliced avocado and refried beans to make a more substantial meal.

I'm really not one for name-dropping but... kedgeree always reminds me of Sir Christopher Lee. I was lucky enough to work with him when I was 22. We did a film together called *A Feast at Midnight*. Fittingly, the film was all about food being the way to a young girl's heart... We stayed at a lovely pub while we were filming and every morning Christopher and I had breakfast together. I would always order boiled eggs but I remember he ate many different things, including kedgeree. So in honour of this lovely man, I give you kedgeree!

Kedgeree

SERVES 4–6

500 g (1 lb) naturally dyed smoked haddock

250 g (8 oz) basmati or long-grain rice, rinsed in cold water

500 ml (17 fl oz) chicken or fish stock

3 eggs

1 tablespoon butter

4 spring onions, finely sliced

100 g (3½ oz) frozen peas, defrosted

finely grated zest and juice of 1 lemon

150 ml (¼ pint) crème fraîche

salt and pepper

a small handful of fresh parsley

To cook the haddock, place it in a large frying pan, skin side up, and pour over enough water to cover. Bring to a simmer and poach the fish for around 10 minutes or until the flesh flakes easily.

Drain and, when cool, pick out any bones and skin to leave nice big fish flakes.

In the meantime, put the rice into a saucepan with the stock, cover with a lid and bring to the boil. Reduce the heat to a simmer and cook gently for about 10 minutes. Remove from the heat, uncover and leave to stand for about 5 minutes more, by which time all the stock should have been absorbed.

While this is happening, put the eggs in a saucepan of cold water, bring to the boil and cook for 8–10 minutes. Drain them under cold running water and, when cool enough, remove the shells, cut into quarters and set aside.

Melt the butter in a large frying pan and gently soften the spring onions for a few minutes. Stir through the rice, peas, lemon zest and crème fraîche and cook for 3–4 minutes, checking for seasoning and adding some salt and black pepper if needed.

Add the fish flakes and parsley to the pan along with the lemon juice (you may only need half). Taste again to check the seasoning. Serve garnished with the egg quarters.

When I worked in the top floor restaurant at Smiths of Smithfield, the boys in the kitchen would take it in turns to make breakfast (that is if we had time). It ranged from scrambled eggs or just sausages to vanilla porridge. I'm not usually a fan of porridge, I can take it or leave it, but when one of the chefs made this it was so super-creamy and delicious that I felt a little like Goldilocks and ate three bowlfuls!

Vanilla porridge

SERVES 4

200 g (7 oz) porridge oats

750 ml (1¼ pints) full-fat milk

250 ml (8 fl oz) double cream

2 vanilla pods, seeds scraped and pods too

a good pinch of salt

maple syrup or vanilla sugar, to serve

Put the porridge oats, milk, cream and vanilla seeds and pods into a saucepan over a medium heat. Bring just to the boil, stirring constantly.

Once bubbling, add the salt and cook for about 4–5 minutes. Discard the vanilla pods and serve with a little maple syrup or vanilla sugar.

Sometimes I want a full-on fry-up for breakfast... usually I want just a boiled egg... but there are days when I am in a rush, trying to get Billie ready for school and myself ready for work, and I just don't seem to have the time to sit down, so I often end up taking breakfast with me. This consists of my travel mug of Earl Grey tea and a disposable cup left over from one of Billie's parties filled with yogurt and granola.

I never realised granola was so easy to make. What is lovely about it is that you can substitute whatever nuts, seeds or grains you like and add dried fruit if you want to. There are a lot of ingredients but a batch should last you a while. This is my version of a classic breakfast.

Granola

MAKES ABOUT 1 KG (2 LB)

450 g (14½ oz) porridge oats

200 g (7 oz) almonds, chopped

100 g (3½ oz) mixed nuts, chopped

100 g (3½ oz) sesame seeds

75 g (3 oz) roasted hazelnuts, chopped

50 g (2 oz) sunflower seeds

50 g (2 oz) pumpkin seeds

125 g (4 oz) soft brown sugar

1 teaspoon ground ginger

1 teaspoon sea salt

175 g (6 oz) fruit purée (I use unsweetened apple sauce) or fruit juice

100 g (3½ oz) maple syrup

75 g (3 oz) honey

2 teaspoons vanilla extract

2 tablespoons vegetable oil

Preheat the oven to 150°C (300°F), gas mark 2.

Mix all of the dry ingredients together in a large bowl.

Warm the fruit purée or juice, maple syrup, honey, vanilla extract and oil in a saucepan over a low heat.

Mix the wet mixture into the dry until thoroughly combined and then tip the mixture on to 2–3 baking trays (with sides) depending on the size. Bake in the preheated oven for 50 minutes, turning the mixture over every 10 minutes.

Leave the baked granola to cool and dry completely and then put in an airtight container. It will keep for at least a month.

I have done quite a bit of work with Florida grapefruit. It's funny because I'm not particularly a fan of the standard variety but these pink grapefruit are so juicy and much sweeter than the others. I came up with a smoothie recipe for them, which is delicious, and I have included a couple of others too. They are the perfect breakfast when we are rushing around in the morning. I cut all the fruit up the night before then bung all the ingredients in a blender and there is my breakfast in a glass.

Smoothies

1 Florida grapefruit

1 banana

100 ml (3½ fl oz) Greek-style yogurt

1–2 tablespoons honey

fresh mint leaves, to decorate (optional)

GRAPEFRUIT SMOOTHIE

Cut the grapefruit in half and then cut a slice about 1 cm (½ inch) thick – this will be used for decoration later. Remove the skin from the rest of the grapefruit and place the fruit into a medium-sized jug.

Roughly chop the banana and add it to the grapefruit along with the yogurt and whizz with a hand-held blender. This can also be done in a blender or smoothie maker.

Add the honey to taste and whizz again. Taste the mixture – if you prefer it slightly sweeter, then add more honey.

Pour the liquid into glasses or bottles, decorate with the sliced grapefruit and mint if liked and serve immediately.

175 g (6 oz) blueberries

1 banana

125 ml (4 fl oz) Greek-style yogurt

125 ml (4 fl oz) apple juice

BLUEBERRY SMOOTHIE

Put all the ingredients in a food processor, blender or smoothie maker and blitz until smooth. Serve in tall glasses or bottles.

2 mangos

250 ml (8 fl oz) milk

2 tablespoons honey

MANGO SMOOTHIE

Put all the ingredients in a food processor, blender or smoothie maker and blitz until smooth. Serve in tall glasses or bottles.

I couldn't do a Sunday morning chapter and not include my perfect Bloody Mary. When I was in my 20s and 30s these were weekend regulars. Angela, Nicola and I used to have this hangover 'sigh' – we would have a sip of Bloody Mary and then let out a heavenly sigh that meant it's all okay! Now I am a 40-year-old mother and these moments are less frequent, but I've got to say I still love them. I like a real kick to mine; I have included a guide as to how to prepare them but feel free to play around with how much of the ingredients you want to add. Also, we don't really go a lot for ice in this country, but really what this beauty of a drink needs is lashings of it.

Bloody Mary

SERVES 4
100 ml (3½ fl oz) vodka (or however much you would like to put in!)
1 litre (1¾ pints) tomato juice
juice of 1 lemon
juice of 1 lime
1 teaspoon Worcestershire sauce
1 teaspoon horseradish sauce
1 teaspoon Tabasco
1 teaspoon celery salt
celery sticks and lemon wedges or twists, to serve

Throw a lot of ice in a large jug and pour over the vodka, tomato juice, lemon and lime juices and the spices. Mix really well and serve with a stick of celery and a wedge of lemon… and sigh!

on Rainy Days

I'm with Karen Carpenter on this one — rainy days do get me down... though for me it's also Sundays, not Mondays, as I've already explained! So rainy days to me are days of comfort food and watching films, but mostly they are about baking. I'm not very good at being shut indoors for long periods of time; I like to be out doing stuff, and the only way I cope with being inside with the rain hammering down and the grey skies outside is by making things that make people smile – baking cakes and cooking pies, but also making presents (food of course!). So jams, preserved lemons, jars of pears. It's really a chapter about how to cheer myself up, and in doing that making other people happy, and I hope it does that to you too.

This is a recipe from my teenage years. For a little while I was a right old hippy (or I thought I was!), hanging out with bands, wearing dungarees, being a veggie... and raving! Well, it *was* 1990! I used to be friends with a gorgeous girl called Holly who I thought was so cool. She lived in Devon and smoked roll-ups and wore clogs and had beautiful tapestry bags. My sister and I were fascinated by her. She could also cook, and one of the things she used to make was homity pie. I remember thinking she seemed so relaxed and confident in her own skin and I was completely the opposite, I tried to take a leaf out of her book, but I think I only came away with this recipe!

This is called a 'pie', but it is actually more like a quiche as it has no lid.

Homity pie

SERVES 6–8

1 quantity Shortcrust Pastry (see page 9)

flour, for dusting

400 g (13 oz) potatoes, peeled

60 g (2¼ oz) butter

1 thyme stalk

4 small–medium onions, finely sliced

2 garlic cloves, finely sliced

100 g (3½ oz) Cheddar cheese, grated

150 ml (¼ pint) double cream

2 teaspoons mustard powder

salt and pepper

Preheat the oven to 200°C (400°F), gas mark 6. Roll out the pastry on a lightly floured surface and use it to line a 25-cm (10-inch) pie or tart case. Bake blind in the preheated oven for about 15 minutes. Remove the baking beans, prick the base with a fork and bake for another 5 minutes.

Meanwhile, boil the potatoes in a large saucepan of water until tender and then chop into small cubes.

While the potatoes are boiling, melt the butter in a frying pan over a low heat, add the thyme and slowly soften the onions and garlic (I cook these really slowly so they become soft and sweet and slightly caramelised).

Add the cooked cubed potatoes and cheese to the onions and then add the cream, mustard powder and season with some salt and pepper.

Pour into the blind-baked pastry case and cook for a further 15 minutes until the top is golden. Serve with a green salad.

I have only ever had proper meatloaf once and it was in Washington DC at a little restaurant in Georgetown. I love the name of it and the all-American idea of it. Growing up, I was pretty obsessed with American films and loved seeing the houses and the food and the fact that everyone drank iced tea or milk and had salad with most of their dinners and mashed potatoes – the things you remember! Anyway, meatloaf was a firm movie favourite, and when I was over in the States filming for *This Morning* I asked a butcher what he put in his meatloaf, then came home and experimented. This is what I came up with – a perfect recipe for a rainy afternoon.

Meatloaf

SERVES 4

1 large onion, very finely chopped

1 garlic clove, finely chopped

1–2 red chillies, deseeded and finely chopped

2 celery sticks, finely chopped

1 green pepper, deseeded and finely chopped

75 g (3 oz) fresh or dried breadcrumbs

1 large egg

1 tablespoon soy sauce

1 teaspoon Dijon mustard

a good dash of Worcestershire sauce

450 g (14½ oz) minced beef

450 g (14½ oz) minced pork

salt and pepper

Note: This is easiest to make in a food processor, but it can all be mixed by hand in a bowl if necessary.

Preheat the oven to 180°C (350°F), gas mark 4.

Put the onion, garlic, chillies and celery in a food processor and blitz until fine. Add the green pepper, breadcrumbs, egg, soy sauce, mustard and Worcestershire sauce and pulse until combined.

Tip the contents out into a big bowl and mix, using your hands, with the minced beef and pork so that all of the ingredients are evenly combined. Season with some black pepper and add a little salt if needed (the soy is quite salty!).

Pack the mix into a 1 kg (2 lb) loaf tin or an enamel pie dish and press down well. Stand the tin in a roasting tray and pour hot water from the kettle into the tray until it comes halfway up the sides of the loaf tin.

Bake in the preheated oven for 50–60 minutes or until the loaf shrinks from the sides of the tin and the juices run clear when you insert a skewer.

Leave the loaf to rest for 10–15 minutes as it will be easier to cut when cooler.

I remember Billie and I going round to Nicola's house one rainy Sunday afternoon. I moped in like a moody teenager, berating the rain and the gloomy 'Sundayness' of life, only to be greeted by a calm and smiling Nicola, a sleeping baby on her shoulder and the most enticing smell coming from her kitchen. Now, anybody who knows my best friend will understand that this domestic little scene is not the norm… that's not to say it's always chaos, but Nicola and her lovely family do tend to bumble around a bit, and the fact that she was so happy that she had cooked something she had made up herself was so infectious that my silly mood was soon forgotten – and that was before I'd even tasted her dish, which was so delicious and rainy-Sunday-blues-banishing that it had to be included!

Nicola's sausages with apples & thyme

SERVES 4–6

1 tablespoon olive oil

8 good-quality sausages

1 large onion, sliced

500 g (1 lb) floury potatoes, washed and cut into wedges

2 eating apples, cored and cut into wedges

200 ml (7 fl oz) chicken stock

2–3 fresh thyme sprigs

Preheat the oven to 190°C (375°F), gas mark 5.

Heat the olive oil in a large frying pan and cook the sausages for a couple of minutes until browned. Remove from the pan and set aside.

In the same pan, fry the onion until softened and then add the potatoes and apples and cook for a few more minutes.

Place everything in an ovenproof dish, with about 150 ml (¼ pint) of the stock and the thyme. Cover with foil and cook in the preheated oven for 30 minutes.

After 30 minutes remove the foil, add more stock if the mixture seems to need it (if it is sticking to the pan/drying up a little). Return to the oven for a further 15–20 minutes, until everything is golden brown and cooked through and the potatoes are tender. Remove the thyme sprigs before serving.

Potted shrimps remind me of my granddad, Norman. He was very strict and was always telling us off for having our elbows on the table or talking with our mouths full. He was a very quiet, private man, and he always carried a bag of 'stuff' around with him. My sister and my cousins and I thought that he was some sort of spy and we used to try and steal the bag and look through it! I remember one day we planned a whole 'Get The Bag' mission and actually brought said bag up to our room, only to find a load of letters and papers that meant nothing to us. Still, I remember we logged it in a book and called ourselves the 4D Special Agents. Anyway I digress... He loved potted shrimps and I used to watch in awe as he spread these tiny pink and yellow things on crunchy toast. I was always too scared of him to ask for a taste, but as I grew up they were one of the first things I tried at a restaurant. I have also included potted cheese here, as it's so easy and makes a really nice supper or a lovely gift.

Potted shrimps & potted cheese

SERVES 4
200 g (7 oz) unsalted butter
a pinch of salt
a pinch of nutmeg
a pinch of cayenne pepper
a squeeze of lemon juice
400 g (13 oz) peeled brown shrimps

Melt the butter in a saucepan over a low heat and add the salt, spices and lemon juice. Stir through the shrimps and spoon into 4 x 150 ml (¼ pint) ramekin or glass dishes, topping up with a little more of the butter.

Transfer the ramekin dishes to the fridge to set and remove 10 minutes before serving. Serve with Melba toast.

VARIATION: POTTED CHEESE

Mix 200 g (7 oz) cheese (I like to use a Stilton or a crunchy Cheddar – a good strong one works best), 50 g (2 oz) softened butter, a splash of Worcestershire sauce, a pinch of mustard powder and 2–3 tablespoons sherry together in a bowl until smooth – I use a hand-held electric whisk. Put the mixture into little jars or ramekin dishes and seal with melted butter. Refrigerate.

When I go out to eat, I'm usually starving and excited about trying a new restaurant, or going to a tried and tested place, and the last thing I want to fill up on is bread. However, sometimes it is too good to resist, and last year I went out for dinner and the only memorable thing was the ginger and rosemary bread. I came home and had the perfect opportunity one rainy afternoon to start playing around with it until I'd come up with my own version. Billie loves it warm with honey, but it's great on its own or toasted.

Rosemary & ginger bread

MAKES 2 LOAVES

500 g (1 lb) strong white flour, plus extra for dusting

10 g (¼ oz) salt

250 ml (8 fl oz) warm water

1 x 7 g sachet dried yeast

2 tablespoons honey

1 teaspoon oil

1 tablespoon freshly chopped rosemary

2.5 cm (1 inch) piece of fresh ginger, coarsely grated

Note: To get a better crust, as with the Sourdough (see page 92), place a baking tray in the bottom of the oven and pour in a little cold water or some ice cubes when you first put the bread in.

Combine the flour and the salt in a large bowl. Mix the warm water in a jug with the yeast, honey and oil. Make a well in the centre of the flour, gradually add the water and mix together with your hands until it forms a pliable dough.

Using a stand mixer and dough hook, or just your good old-fashioned hands, knead the dough for about 10 minutes, until you get the windowpane effect (see page 92). Add the rosemary and grated ginger and knead again, a little more slowly, until combined.

Put the dough in a lightly oiled bowl with a clean damp tea towel over the top and leave until it has virtually doubled in size, which takes about an hour or so.

Take the dough out of the bowl and punch the air out of it, or 'knock it back', as they say. Cut the dough in half, shape into 2 balls and put each in a floured tea towel and leave again for about an hour. Meanwhile, preheat the oven to 230°C (450°F), gas mark 8.

Put the bread into the preheated oven for 10 minutes, then turn the heat down to 200°C (400°F), gas mark 6 and cook for a further 20 minutes until golden brown and the base sounds hollow when tapped.

When I was a child it was never the chocolate biscuits that I went for – it was always the shortbread.
I loved the buttery and sweet biscuit that had a slight saltiness to it, and today it's still my favourite.

I recently met and worked with a great baker called Patrick Ryan. When we did an online how-to-cook series for the BBC, he taught me how to make the best sourdough I have ever tasted and also gave me his starter. Up until *MasterChef* I'd never even heard of a starter… however, with *MasterChef* came confidence and with confidence came a load of wonderful experiences working with amazing chefs and thus more confidence, which resulted in me truly believing I could make sourdough. And, honestly, you can too!

Now, the whole starter thing – this is used instead of yeast and is where your sourdough gets its flavour from. You can ask your local baker or you can make one yourself. It's SO easy; the only faff is feeding it once a week. AND you can also freeze it!

A quick thought before I go on with the recipe: sourdough does take up quite a bit of time, so is perfect for a rainy day. Let it prove overnight and bake it the next morning… it's honestly worth all the effort. This is Patrick's amazing recipe!

Sourdough

MAKES 2 LOAVES

500 g (1 lb) strong bread flour

1 quantity Sourdough Starter (see page 11)

250 ml (8 fl oz) water

10 g (¼ oz) brown sugar

10 g (¼ oz) salt

Notes: If you have a food processor fitted with a dough hook, this will take no time at all.

To get the windowpane effect with your dough, hold the dough up to the window or the light and you should be able to see through it without it breaking. It should be stretchy and look like a shammy leather.

Mix together the flour, starter and water in a bowl. Add the sugar and salt and knead for about 10 minutes, or put in a stand mixer with dough hook for 10 minutes, until the windowpane effect is achieved (see Notes).

Lightly oil a bowl, place the dough in, cover with a clean damp tea towel and leave to prove for 2–3 hours (it will not rise anywhere near as much as dough with yeast in).

Turn out the dough and knock the air out of it. Cut in half and shape into 2 balls. Flour them, wrap them in a heavily floured tea towel and put them in bowls. Leave for another 2 hours at least (usually I put them in the fridge overnight and then bake them in the morning, but take them out of the fridge for at least 30 minutes before baking). Preheat the oven to 230°C (450°F), gas mark 8.

Put the bread on a baking tray, score and place in the preheated oven. Place another baking tray with a few ice cubes in the bottom of the oven to create steam, and bake for 35–40 minutes until a good crust has formed. I like to serve this toasted with a soft-boiled egg on top.

After writing my first recipe book, Recipes from my Mother for my Daughter, my auntie Susan called me up and said that she was so proud of me, that she had just come across my grandma Betty's recipe book, and that out of all in the family she thought it should go to me. I was very touched and also very excited when said recipe book arrived at my door. It has all my grandma's cakes, pies and sauces, as well as some proper old-school cuttings from magazines in the early 60s. Now, Betty used to make an AMAZING ginger cake, really sticky and sweet and just like the Jamaican ginger cake you get in the shops (but nicer, of course, because it's homemade). You can imagine my excitement when I found her recipe written in the book! Here it is.

Ginger cake

MAKES 1 LARGE LOAF

225 g (7½ oz) unbleached white self-raising flour

1 teaspoon bicarbonate of soda

1 tablespoon ground ginger

1 teaspoon ground cinnamon

1 teaspoon ground mixed spice

110 g (3½ oz) cold unsalted butter, cut into cubes

110 g (3½ oz) black treacle

110 g (3½ oz) golden syrup

110 g (3½ oz) light muscovado sugar

280 ml (9 fl oz) milk

1 egg, beaten

vegetable oil, for greasing

Preheat the oven to 180°C (350°F), gas mark 4. Grease and base line a 900 g (2 lb) loaf tin.

Sift all the dry ingredients, except the sugar, into a large mixing bowl. Rub in the butter with your fingertips until the mixture resembles fine crumbs.

Melt the treacle with the syrup in a saucepan over a medium heat and then leave to cool to blood temperature. Meanwhile, dissolve the sugar in the milk in a saucepan over a low heat, stirring. Whisk the milk into the flour mixture and then whisk in the treacle mixture followed by the egg. When all is thoroughly combined, the mixture will be like a thin batter.

Pour the mixture into the prepared tin. Bake for 40–45 minutes, until a skewer inserted into the centre comes out clean. During baking the mixture will rise, then sink. Leave to cool completely in the tin, then turn out and peel off the lining paper. Wrap in greaseproof paper and then foil and keep for a couple of days before slicing.

It's very fitting as I sit here and write this that tomorrow is the Queen's Diamond Jubilee. Thirty-five years ago, in 1977, it was her Silver Jubilee. I remember dressing up as the Queen of Hearts for our street party, where everybody wore red, white and blue. My outfit was made of crêpe paper and I was carrying my mum's homemade jam tarts... Tonight, as I get Billie's Union Jack 'prom dress' ready and make a dish of coronation chicken and some jam tarts for nostalgia's sake, I am transported back to my five-year-old self.

Jam tarts

MAKES 12 TARTS

150 g (5 oz) butter or margarine

300 g (10 oz) plain flour, plus extra for dusting

a pinch of salt

1–2 tablespoons water

strawberry and apricot jam

Preheat the oven to 190°C (375°F), gas mark 5. Grease a 12-hole bun tray.

Make the pastry by putting the butter, flour and salt in a food processor and pulsing until the mixture resembles breadcrumbs. Alternatively, you can make this by hand by rubbing the ingredients together with your fingertips.

Add the water until it comes together and then form the pastry into a ball. Cover with cling film and transfer to the fridge for at least 30 minutes to rest.

Roll out the pastry on a lightly floured surface to about 1 cm (½ inch) thick and use a 6 cm (2½ inch) cutter to cut out 12 tarts.

Put the pastry circles in the prepared bun tray and bake blind in the preheated oven for 5–10 minutes.

Take out of the oven and spoon the jam into the pastry cases. Return to the oven for a further 10 minutes.

When I was a child it was never the chocolate biscuits that I went for – it was always the shortbread. I loved the buttery and sweet biscuit that had a slight saltiness to it, and today it's still my favourite. My grandma used to make it in a flan tin with fork marks around the edges and cut it into triangles, so guess what... I often do the same to cheer up a rainy afternoon!

Proper old-fashioned shortbread

MAKES 8–12 SLICES

175 g (6 oz) plain flour

125 g (4 oz) butter, cubed and at room temperature

50 g (2 oz) caster sugar, plus extra for sprinkling

a good pinch of salt

1 vanilla pod, seeds scraped

Preheat the oven to 190°C (375°F), gas mark 5 and grease a 23 cm (9 inch) tart tin.

Put all the ingredients into a food processor and pulse until it forms a dough. Alternatively, mix by hand in a bowl. Roll out to a circle that fits the tin, taking care not to over-handle the shortbread. Press the mixture into the tin and fork the edges.

Bake in the preheated oven for 30–35 minutes until golden.

As soon as the shortbread is out of the oven, cut it into 8–12 segments and fork holes in the top. Leave to cool in the tin. When cool, sprinkle with sugar.

When I was in New York filming I got to go to the famous Magnolia Bakery and cook with the chief baking officer, Bobbie Lloyd. I was desperate to put a proper all-American cream pie recipe in my book... so who better to ask than Bobbie herself? This will bring sunshine and a 'have a nice day' smile to your rainy day.

Banana cream pie

MAKES A 23 CM (9 INCH) PIE

FOR THE PIE BASE

100 g (3½ oz) unsalted butter, plus extra for greasing

225–275 g (7½ –9 oz) digestive biscuits, crushed

25 g (1 oz) caster sugar

FOR THE FILLING

175 g (6 oz) caster sugar

4 tablespoons cornflour

¼ teaspoon salt

825 ml (29 fl oz) milk

4 large egg yolks

60 g (2 oz) softened butter

2 teaspoons vanilla extract

3 ripe bananas, sliced (reserving a couple of slices for decoration)

FOR THE TOPPING

450 ml (¾ pint) whipped cream

2 teaspoons icing sugar

½ teaspoon vanilla extract

Preheat the oven to 180°C (350°F), gas mark 4. Butter a 23 cm (9 inch) pie dish. To make the pie base, melt the butter in a saucepan or the microwave and then set it aside to cool. Add the biscuit crumbs and the sugar to the butter and stir until fully mixed.

Place the crumb mixture into your buttered pie dish and press firmly with the back of a spoon on the base and up the sides to form a 5 mm (¼ inch) edge. You can place a piece of cling film over the biscuit base at this point and, using another pie dish, press the crumbs to flatten. Bake the pie base in the preheated oven for about 8 minutes and then leave to cool completely before you fill it.

Make the filling: whisk the sugar, cornflour and salt in a heavy-based pan until all incorporated. Continue to whisk as you gradually add the milk. Whisk in the yolks, stirring vigorously until no flecks of yolk appear. Place the pan over a medium heat and bring to the boil, stirring constantly with a whisk. When it reaches a full boil, reduce to a low heat and stir for about 3 minutes. Strain the mixture into a bowl. Beat in the butter and vanilla. Cover with greaseproof paper and cool for 15 minutes. Remove the paper and stir well.

Layer half the sliced bananas on the prepared crust. Pour half the cream filling on top and then add the rest of the bananas and the rest of the filling. Cover with cling film directly on the filling and chill for at least 4 hours until set.

To make the topping, beat the cream, icing sugar and vanilla together in a bowl until soft peaks form. Spread the cream over the pie with a spatula and decorate with banana slices.

I first made these pears for a dinner party a few years ago. They looked beautiful and were a real hit! If you are cooking them, and not preserving them, make the mulled wine first and then poach the pears in that, covered with a circle of greaseproof paper, for 40 minutes until tender. If the day is a washout you can preserve the pears: first make up the wine, then put the pears into the jars, pour the wine over and cook them in the jars in the oven – they make lovely gifts. The smell of them cooking will instantly put you in a better mood and they are perfect served with a shortbread biscuit (see page 98) and a dollop of mascarpone.

Poached pears in mulled wine

MAKES 2 JARS
1 lemon, halved

4 pears

FOR THE MULLED WINE
grated zest and juice of 1 orange

grated zest and juice of 1 lemon

grated zest and juice of 1 lime

225 g (7½ oz) caster sugar

6 cloves

1 cinnamon stick

3 bay leaves

1 whole nutmeg, grated

1 vanilla pod

1 bottle red wine

YOU WILL NEED
2 sterilised Kilner jars

Put all the mulled wine ingredients into a pan, bring to the boil and simmer for 10 minutes until the sugar has dissolved.

Meanwhile, squeeze the halved lemon into a bowl of cold water. Peel the pears and, as you peel each one, place it straight into the bowl of lemon water.

Add the pears to the simmering wine and then remove the pan from the heat. Take a large sheet of greaseproof paper, scrunch it up and press on to the pears to keep them submerged. Cover the pan with a lid and leave for 1–1½ hours until tender.

Remove the pears from the liquid and set aside. Bring the wine to the boil and then boil vigorously for 10–12 minutes until the liquid reduces by one-third and is syrupy. Strain the liquid. Place the pears into sterilised jars, pour over the liquid and seal.

Store in a cool, dark place for up to 3 months.

This Christmas pudding recipe has been in my family for years. I thought it was a lovely recipe to be able to include in my 'rainy days' chapter because it doesn't matter when you make them, they last for ages, and the longer you keep them the better they taste. Also, I like to make them in bulk, for my friends and relatives. I don't have a big enough bowl to mix the fruit and usually end up using my kitchen sink!

My family's Christmas pudding

THIS MAKES 3 PUDDINGS
– 1.5 KG (3 LB) + 1 KG
(2 LB) + 500 G (1 LB) OR THE
COMBINATION OF YOUR CHOICE

125 g (4 oz) plain flour

500 g (1 lb) shredded suet

500 g (1 lb) stoned raisins

500 g (1 lb) mixed fruit

500 g (1 lb) currants

500 g (1 lb) caster sugar

125 g (4 oz) cherries

125 g (4 oz) chopped almonds (optional)

2 whole nutmegs, grated (or 2 rounded teaspoons ground nutmeg)

2 level teaspoons mixed spice

finely grated zest and juice of 1 lemon

finely grated zest and juice of 1 orange

8 eggs, beaten

150 ml (¼ pint) brandy

75 ml (3 fl oz) sherry

Put all the ingredients except the eggs, brandy and sherry, into a large mixing bowl and stir. Mix in the eggs, brandy and sherry and stir well.

Put the mixture into your basins – 1 x 1.5 kg (3 lb), 1 x 1 kg (2 lb) and 1 x 500 g (1 lb), or your chosen combination.

Cover with muslin or foil and steam in a large saucepan for 6 hours, topping up regularly with boiling water. The mixture changes to a darker brown and smells delicious when cooked.

Store, wrapped in foil or greaseproof paper, until Christmas. Boil or steam for 2 hours before eating.

The puddings will keep for a good 10 months if stored, well wrapped, in a cool, dark place.

Blackcurrant jam is one of the simplest jams to make because it sets so easily. Every time I make it I wish that I could bottle the smell. When it's raining outside and all my clean jars are lined up and I'm spooning homemade jam into them, I can actually manage to crack a smile!

Blackcurrant jam

MAKES ABOUT 5 KG (10 LB)

2 kg (4 lb) blackcurrants

juice of 1 lemon

1.8 litres (3 pints) water

3 kg (6 lb) granulated sugar

a knob of butter

Tip: This jam is best served with 'drop scones'. These are also called Scotch pancakes and the recipe is the same as for the American Pancakes on page 58. Just use a dessertspoonful of the pancake batter to make a small scone-sized pancake and then enjoy them with the jam.

Put the blackcurrants (make sure all the little stalks are removed), lemon juice and water in a large preserving pan and set over a medium heat. Bring to the boil and then simmer for about 40 minutes.

Add the sugar and dissolve slowly over a low heat, stirring all the time.

Once the sugar has dissolved, turn up the heat and keep it on a rolling boil for about 10 minutes.

Test for a set: put a teaspoon of the jam on a cold saucer; if the jam wrinkles when you push it with your finger then it is ready. If it doesn't, continue cooking for another 5–10 minutes and then test again. Stir in the knob of butter, which should remove any scum on the top and then spoon the jam into sterilised jars.

Store in a cool, dark place for up to a year.

The flavour of preserved lemons is quite intense, but delicate at the same time. Essentially they are just pickled in salt and their own juice. They are a lovely ingredient to use and really bring an extra dimension to some recipes. Slice the zest thinly and stir through mashed or crushed potatoes and serve with fish or chicken, or put in a tagine. As I mention in my tagine recipe (see page 36), a very dear friend gave me a jar of these as a gift. I thought they were beautiful, so what better way to spend a rainy day than to make gifts for people you love...

Preserved lemons

MAKES 2 X 1 LITRE
(1¼ PINT) JARS

12 lemons – 6 for the jar and 6 for their juice

250 g (8 oz) sea salt

4 bay leaves

6 peppercorns

1 teaspoon coriander seeds (optional)

Note: When you want to use the lemon, take it out and rinse off the salt, scoop out the pith and just use the thin delicate skin.

Cut 6 of the lemons in quarters lengthways, but not all the way to the top, so that they still hold together (do this over a bowl to preserve any juice). Squeeze the 6 other lemons and reserve the juice.

Put a good tablespoon of salt in the bottom of each sterilised jar, then pack the quartered lemons with salt and push them tightly together into the jars. Divide the bay leaves, peppercorns and coriander seeds, if using, between the jars and cover with the squeezed lemon juice and remaining salt. If the juice doesn't cover the lemons then top up with water.

Close the jars and shake. Make sure that there is a layer of salt at the bottom. Every day for 2 weeks turn the jars and add salt if necessary. They are ready to use after about a month but the longer you leave them, the better they taste. They will keep for up to a year if stored in a cool, dark place.

This is a taste that transports me straight back to my grandma Betty's kitchen. She made all sorts of jams, but my absolute favourite was crab apple jelly – it was the most beautiful colour. I remember putting the jar on the windowsill and looking through the jelly/jam, which bathed the garden in a pinky-peachy glow! I loved the sharpness of it too. I don't know if it's because I live in London, but I hardly ever see crab apples. They are in season in September I think, and are quite hard to come by, but if you or anyone you know has a crab apple tree in your garden then grab them and make this delicious jam.

Crab apple jelly

MAKES JUST OVER 1 KG (2 LB)
1.5 kg (3 lb) crab apples
1.2 litres (2 pints) water
grated zest of 1 lemon
granulated sugar

Put the apples in a large preserving pan and cover with the water. Add the lemon zest and bring to the boil. Cover and simmer for about 30–40 minutes until the crab apples are really soft and squidgy.

Pour the apples into a jelly bag and leave to drip over a bowl overnight. Do not be tempted to squeeze the bag because it will make the jelly cloudy not clear!

Measure how much juice you have and then add 500 g (1 lb) granulated sugar to every 600 ml (1 pint) juice. Put the juice and sugar into a preserving pan and slowly bring to the boil. Keep stirring until the sugar has dissolved.

Cook at a rolling boil for about 5–10 minutes, and then test to see if it has set – put a teaspoon of the jelly on a cold saucer; if the jelly wrinkles when you push it with your finger then it is ready. If it doesn't, coninue cooking for another 5–10 minutes and then test again.

Once set, pour into sterilised jars. Store in a cool, dark place for up to a year.

This is a winner whatever the weather. But if you are not as cooking-obsessed as me, when it's too wet to venture outside, why not hunker down, watch your favourite film and snuggle up with a great big bowl of popcorn!

Salted toffee popcorn

MAKES ENOUGH FOR A FAMILY FILM NIGHT OR A FAMILY FILM ON A RAINY DAY!

I tablespoon vegetable oil

150 g (5 oz) popcorn kernels

100 g (3½ oz) caster sugar

75 ml (3 fl oz) water

a generous pinch of sea salt flakes

75 g (3 oz) unsalted butter

Heat the oil in a large, heavy-based saucepan over a high heat. Add the popcorn kernels and quickly cover with a lid. Cook, shaking at regular intervals, for 4–5 minutes or until the popping has stopped.

Pour the popcorn into a large bowl and set aside. Wipe out any excess bits of popcorn from the pan and return to the heat. Pour in the sugar, water and salt and return to the heat. Cook, without stirring, for 2–3 minutes, until the sugar has melted and starts to turn a deep caramel colour. Stir in the butter (it will sizzle, but not for long) and keep stirring until the caramel is smooth and glossy. Return the popcorn to the pan and stir until evenly coated.

Spread the popcorn out in an even layer over a couple of baking trays and leave to cool for 20 minutes. Transfer to a large bowl and serve.

THE WAY I COOK...

when I Have no Time

Now this is tricky! People often ask me for 'quick dishes', and my sister (my voice of reason) always laughs because she says that not everybody is as obsessed by cooking as me and that, because I love it, I spend way more time in the kitchen than most. Well, what I wanted to do here was write a chapter that isn't necessarily just 30-minute meals, but also one-pot dishes that could be put in the oven and forgotten about. To me, it's not always about being fast; it's also that you will more often than not have other stuff to do while the dinner is cooking. I've also included some dishes in here, which, although quick, are still pretty special.

Mussels were always a dish that I would order at a restaurant, but never even thought about making at home. I don't know why... Well, I do – it's a confidence thing. But they really are very easy, and great served with either crusty bread or skinny chips. Also, these are one of Billie's favourite things to eat; she loves using the empty mussel shell as 'pincers' to pick out the other mussels, so it really is a good dish for all the family!

Mussels in white wine with shallots & garlic

SERVES 4

1 kg (2 lb) mussels

25 g (1 oz) butter

4 shallots, finely diced

175 ml (6 fl oz) white wine or dry cider

175 ml (6 fl oz) double cream

a handful of fresh flat-leaf parsley, roughly chopped

salt and pepper

Wash the mussels thoroughly, removing any beards or barnacles and discarding any that are open.

Melt the butter in a large saucepan over a medium heat and fry the shallots until soft. Add the wine (or cider) and cream and bring briefly to the boil. Add the mussels, put a lid on the pan and give it a good shake to move the sauce around the mussels. Season with salt and pepper.

Turn the heat down and leave the mussels to steam for about 5 minutes, until they are open. Shake the pan every so often while they cook as they open better that way.

Transfer the mussels to a serving dish using a slotted spoon, discarding any that remain closed. Taste the sauce to see if it needs any more seasoning and add the parsley. Pour the sauce over the mussels and serve with crusty bread or skinny chips.

This is just a guide for a quick dinner, starting with a soup and adding bits of what you fancy to make it more substantial. Feel free to play around with it...

Miso soup & noodles

SERVES 2–4

2 x 15 g packets of miso soup paste

OTHER INGREDIENTS TO ADD

1 chicken breast, cooked and shredded

8 king prawns, cooked

100 g (3½ oz) tofu, cubed

75 g (3 oz) rice noodles, cooked according to the packet instructions

1 thumb-size piece of fresh ginger, peeled and finely chopped

1 red chilli, deseeded and finely chopped

2–3 spring onions, finely sliced

a small bunch of coriander, leaves torn

Make up the soup following the instructions on the packet.

If adding chicken, prawns, tofu or noodles, heat gently in the soup until piping hot and then garnish with ginger, chilli, spring onions and coriander.

This is one of my wonderful mummy's dinner party dishes that I've tweaked a little. I think she served the prawns in a crêpe – in fact, if my memory serves me correctly, she used to make some sort of layered crêpe and prawn 'cake'. Give it a try if you want to go back to 1982… but I like them on their own with crusty bread.

Prawns in vermouth & cream

SERVES 4

3 tablespoons olive oil

3 shallots, finely sliced

500 g (1 lb) tiger prawns

1 garlic clove, chopped

150 ml (¼ pint) vermouth

juice and grated zest of 1 lemon

75 ml (3 fl oz) double cream

1 tablespoon freshly chopped parsley

salt and pepper

crusty bread, to serve

Heat a frying pan over a medium-high heat. Add the oil, then the shallots and cook for a few minutes. Add the prawns and garlic and cook for a further minute.

Add the vermouth, lemon zest and juice and let this bubble away for 1–2 minutes.

Stir in the cream and then stir through the parsley and season to taste.

Serve with crusty bread.

This is a really quick, easy and tasty dinner. The salmon and prawns cook with the residual heat of the pasta and it is a firm favourite in our house.

Linguine with salmon & prawns

SERVES 4

I shallot, finely chopped

I glass of dry white wine

500 ml (17 fl oz) crème fraîche

2 tablespoons freshly chopped dill

a bunch of fine asparagus (about 6 spears)

400 g (13 oz) linguine

375 g (12 oz) lightly smoked salmon fillets

150 g (5 oz) raw or cooked king prawns

salt and pepper

Put the shallot and wine in a frying pan over a medium heat and bring to the boil. Continue to bubble away until the liquid has reduced by half.

Add the crème fraîche, stir through and then add the dill. Season with salt and pepper

Blanche the asparagus in a saucepan of boiling water for about 30 seconds and then drain.

Cook the linguine in a saucepan of boiling water until al dente and then drain, reserving a little of the pasta water.

Add the creamy sauce to the pasta along with the salmon and prawns. The heat from the pasta and sauce should cook these through but keep over a low heat while stirring to make sure.

Add the asparagus and, if the sauce is too thick, loosen with a little of the pasta water. Serve immediately.

This is a very speedy supper, quick to prepare and to cook. It's a bit of a twist on the usual fish pie and even quicker if you just serve with crusty bread and/or a crisp salad.

Victoria's seafood gratin

SERVES 4

oil, for frying

1 shallot, finely chopped

1 x 400 g tin chopped tomatoes

dash of Tabasco sauce

400 g (13 oz) frozen seafood – e.g. 200 g (7 oz) prawns, 100 g (3½ oz) scallops, 100 g (3½ oz) white fish, or however you want to make it up to the total

100 g (3½ oz) fresh or dried breadcrumbs

1 garlic clove, finely chopped

a handful of fresh parsley, chopped

Preheat the oven to 190°C (375°F), gas mark 5.

Heat a little oil in a large frying pan over a medium heat and fry the shallot until softened. Add the tomatoes, Tabasco sauce and the mixed seafood and cook over a low heat for 2–3 minutes. Transfer the mixture to a large ovenproof dish.

Mix the breadcrumbs, garlic and parsley together in a bowl. Heat a small glug of oil in a pan and toast the breadcrumb mixture for 2–3 minutes, until just starting to turn golden. Sprinkle the breadcrumbs over the seafood mixture.

Bake in the preheated oven for 20–25 minutes until the topping is golden brown and the seafood mixture is piping hot and cooked through.

My sister, Victoria and I bought our first flat together when I was about 25. It had two bedrooms and a little kitchen that looked out on to a communal garden. We absolutely loved it – every Sunday we would completely blitz the place and then settle down on the sofa to watch telly. We took it in turns to cook and this was one of my top things to make.

Baked trout fillets with tomato & fennel

SERVES 4

4 rainbow trout fillets

1 fennel bulb, finely sliced

2 large tomatoes, finely sliced

4 spring onions, finely sliced

1 lemon

butter

salt and pepper

crushed new potatoes, rice or a green salad, to serve

Preheat the oven to 180°C (350°F), gas mark 4. Cut off 4 squares of foil, double the size of the fish fillets.

Divide the fennel between the 4 pieces of foil and place the sliced tomatoes on top. Place the fish on top of the tomatoes, sprinkle with the spring onions and a squeeze of lemon juice, and top with a knob of butter and some salt and pepper.

Fold over the foil and pinch it together to seal, making a pocket that will steam the fish (leave enough room around the fish for the steam to circulate).

Place the foil parcels on a baking tray and cook in the preheated oven for about 10–12 minutes.

Serve with crushed new potatoes, rice or a green salad.

This dish is a real showstopper. The colour is amazing and it makes a great starter or main course.

Beetroot risotto

SERVES 4 AS A MAIN OR 6 AS
A STARTER

I tablespoon olive oil

75 g (3 oz) cold unsalted butter
(50 g (2 oz) of it cubed)

I large onion, peeled and finely
chopped

2 garlic cloves, crushed

300 g (10 oz) Arborio risotto
rice

150 ml (¼ pint) dry white wine

750 ml (1¼ pints) beetroot juice

250 ml (8 fl oz) vegetable stock

2 heaped tablespoons grated
Parmesan cheese

4 small cooked and peeled
beetroot (shop-bought ones
work perfectly), cut into small
cubes

2 tablespoons sherry vinegar

100 g (3½ oz) soft goat's cheese,
crumbled

a small bunch of tarragon,
leaves picked and chopped

salt and pepper

Heat the olive oil and the 25 g (1 oz) uncubed butter in a wide, heavy-based saucepan until the butter is foaming. Add the onion, garlic, a pinch of salt and some black pepper and cook gently for 5 minutes until softened.

Add the rice to the pan and fry for 5 minutes, until the rice starts to turn translucent and smells slightly nutty. Add the wine and boil rapidly, stirring continuously, until the liquid has evaporated. Meanwhile, pour the beetroot juice and vegetable stock into a saucepan and set over a low heat.

Add a ladleful of the hot beetroot stock to the rice and keep stirring until the liquid is almost absorbed. Continue adding the stock, stirring constantly until it has all been incorporated – this will take about 30–35 minutes. The rice should be soft but still have a little bite in the centre.

Remove the pan from the heat and whisk in the cold cubed butter and the Parmesan cheese. Make sure you whisk quite hard so that you work the butter into the rice and end up with a beautifully glossy risotto. Leave the risotto to rest for a couple of minutes.

Meanwhile, put the cubed beetroot and vinegar in a saucepan over a medium heat and simmer gently for a couple of minutes to warm the beetroot through.

Spoon the risotto into warm serving bowls and top with a spoonful of the warm pickled beetroot. Dot some goat's cheese over the top and finish with some chopped tarragon.

Easy peasy and delicious. Honestly, no more words to say...!

Chicken breasts with Parmesan & parsley

SERVES 4

4 chicken breast fillets

4 eggs, beaten

60 g (2½ oz) Parmesan cheese, grated

a handful of fresh parsley, chopped, plus extra for serving

flour, for coating

oil, for frying

60 g (2¼ oz) butter

juice of ½ a lemon

salt and pepper

Wrap the chicken breasts in cling film and flatten with a rolling pin.

Put the beaten eggs, cheese, parsley and some salt and pepper in a bowl and mix together. Put the flour in another bowl. Coat the chicken in flour first, tapping gently to get rid of any excess. Then dip in the egg mixture.

Heat a frying pan with a good glug of oil and fry the coated chicken breasts over a medium-high heat for about 5 minutes on each side. When you have turned the chicken, add the butter. Set the chicken aside to rest for a few minutes.

Add the lemon juice to the buttery oil in the pan to use either as a dressing for a side salad of rocket and watercress, or as a light sauce for some spaghetti which also works well with the chicken. Serve with a sprinkling of extra fresh parsley.

I think the humble chicken Caesar salad is very underrated and it makes a great midweek supper. For the dressing, I was inspired by the very brilliant Mark Sargeant. As I have said before, I feel extremely lucky to have met and been offered advice by some fantastic chefs. Mark made this sauce for me on a cookery show, I loved it and came home and made it for dinner that night!

Chicken Caesar salad with cheat's Caesar dressing

SERVES 4

100 g (3½ oz) cubed pancetta

4 little gem lettuces or a bag of iceberg

100 g (3½ oz) croutons

60 g (2¼ oz) anchovy fillets, sliced

4 cooked chicken breasts, sliced

60 g (2¼ oz) Parmesan, shaved

FOR THE CHEAT'S CAESAR DRESSING

3–4 tablespoons mayonnaise

25 g (1 oz) Parmesan cheese, grated

2 anchovy fillets

1 garlic clove, crushed

a squeeze of lemon juice

To make the dressing, put all of the ingredients in a food processor or blender, blitz until smooth and taste. If the dressing needs loosening, then add a tablespoon at a time of warm water and blitz again.

Fry the pancetta in a frying pan over a medium heat until crispy.

Tear the lettuce and combine in a bowl with the croutons, anchovies, chicken, Parmesan and pancetta, and drizzle over the dressing.

My sister has three children, aged 14, 11 and four, so she is always busy and constantly looking for quick meals to make so she can get on with everything else. This is one she rustled up one day; all the family liked it so it's a regular on their menu now!

Victoria's chicken tray bake

SERVES 4

4 chicken breasts

175 g (6 oz) cherry tomatoes

1 red pepper, deseeded and sliced

about 25 ml (1 fl oz) olive oil (sometimes I like to use a garlic infused one)

25 g (1 oz) fresh or dried breadcrumbs

25 g (1 oz) Parmesan cheese, grated

fresh basil leaves or a sprinkle of dried basil

salt and pepper

buttered new potatoes, to serve

Preheat the oven to 180°C (350°F), gas mark 4.

Simply place the chicken breasts in a shallow ovenproof dish. Add the tomatoes and pepper around the edges. Drizzle over the olive oil and then sprinkle the breadcrumbs over the top, followed by the Parmesan cheese and finally the herbs and some salt and pepper.

Bake in the centre of the preheated oven for 25–30 minutes until cooked through and golden on top.

I like to serve this with buttered baby new potatoes.

I love Mexican food. I first went to Mexico on a modelling job when I was 17 years old and I fell in love with the place. We ate the juiciest mangos by the side of the road, climbed rocks and ate the most delicious street food in the many Mexican markets. There I fell in love with quesadillas. They are so quick, really just a Mexican toasted cheese sandwich, and you can fill them with pretty much anything you like.

Smoked chicken quesadillas

SERVES 4

200 g (7 oz) smoked chicken, shredded

4 spring onions, finely sliced

4 tablespoons pickled jalapeños, sliced

60 g (2¼ oz) sweetcorn

1 tablespoon freshly chopped coriander

125 g (4 oz) Cheddar cheese, grated

4 tablespoons crème fraîche

8 flour tortillas

1 tablespoon oil

salt and pepper

guacamole and soured cream, to serve

Note: If you can't get hold of smoked chicken just use plain cooked chicken instead and add a sprinkling of smoked salt if you have it.

Mix the chicken, spring onions, jalapeños, sweetcorn, coriander, Cheddar, crème fraîche and some salt and pepper together in a bowl.

Spread the mixture evenly between 4 tortillas. Top with the remaining tortillas to make 4 'sandwiches'.

Heat a frying pan and brush a little bit of oil around the pan. Cook the tortilla sandwiches for a few minutes on each side, turning carefully to ensure the filling doesn't escape.

Cut into quarters and serve the quesadillas with guacamole and soured cream.

My mum used to make gammon steaks and jacket potatoes on nights when we had to eat in a hurry, but hers were in true 80s style, topped with pineapple! Years on, I still make that exact dish but I also think this chutney really works with the salty gammon. Oh, and the creamy leek mash adds that little bit of succulent sweetness – the perfect accompaniment.

Gammon steaks with creamy leek mash

SERVES 4

875 g (1¾ lb) potatoes, peeled and diced

50 g (2 oz) butter

2 leeks, sliced

100 ml (3½ fl oz) double cream or milk

1 teaspoon mustard powder

4 unsmoked gammon steaks, weighing about 125 g (4 oz) each

200 g (7 oz) onion chutney

1–2 teaspoons water

salt and pepper

Place the potatoes in a large saucepan of water, bring to the boil, turn down the heat and simmer for 15–20 minutes, until tender.

Melt the butter in a frying pan over a medium heat and fry the leeks for about 5 minutes until softened.

Drain the potatoes and mash. Add the cream or milk and mustard powder and stir, then add the fried leeks and stir well. Season with salt and pepper.

In the frying pan, cook the gammon steaks for a couple of minutes on each side. Add the onion chutney and the water and stir, making sure the gammon is covered in the chutney. Cook for another 3–4 minutes, turning occasionally.

Serve the sticky gammon with the mash.

We have a lot of Greek friends, they are all fantastic cooks, and I am constantly asking for recipes. There always seems to be some family get-together happening and mountains of food being prepared. This is a really quick dish to prepare, a one-pot wonder you can put in the oven and forget about!

Easy Greek lamb

SERVES 4

2 tablespoons olive oil

4 lamb chops or steaks

3–4 sweet potatoes, peeled and cut into wedges

I onion, chopped

500 g (I lb) vine tomatoes, peeled and diced (reserve the juice)

2 tablespoons tomato purée

2 teaspoons ground cumin

2 tablespoons freshly chopped oregano leaves

I teaspoon clear honey

75 ml (3 fl oz) good-quality chicken stock

400 g (13 oz) frozen soya beans

2 tablespoons freshly chopped flat-leaf parsley

I teaspoon lemon juice

salt and pepper

Preheat the oven to 140°C (275°F), gas mark I.

Heat half the oil in a frying pan over a medium heat and brown the lamb. Remove and place in a large ovenproof dish and add the sweet potato wedges.

Using the rest of the oil, fry the onion until softened. Add the tomatoes and their juice and cook for 4–5 minutes. Add the tomato purée, cumin, oregano, honey and chicken stock. Season with salt and pepper and pour this over the lamb and sweet potatoes. Cover with foil and bake in the preheated oven for I hour.

Add the soya beans, cover and cook for another 20 minutes. Stir in the parsley 10 minutes before serving. Remove the foil and stir in the lemon juice. Serve with rice, mashed potatoes or Flatbreads (see page II) for mopping up the juices.

This may seem like a very obvious quick meal, but sometimes those are the things we overlook when in a hurry. It is perfect 'play date' food as it has many variations, with pancetta or without, with peas or without, add sweetcorn or cooked mushrooms, or don't! Use the tomato sauce from my Orecchiette recipe on page 235 if you have some in the freezer or, if really pushed for time, a tub of the fresh supermarket variety. Whatever you decide, I have yet to find a child, or adult for that matter, who doesn't like this super-quick family-friendly dish.

Pasta bake

SERVES 4–6

400 g (13 oz) dried pasta (I like penne for this dish but you can use what you like)

25 g (1 oz) frozen peas (optional)

75 g (3 oz) pancetta, cubed, or bacon lardons (optional)

500 g (1 lb) fresh tomato pasta sauce (shop-bought or see page 235)

125 g (4 oz) mozzarella, cut in pieces

15 g (½ oz) Parmesan cheese

salt and pepper

Preheat the oven to 190°C (375°F), gas mark 5.

Bring a large saucepan of water to the boil and cook the pasta according to the instructions on the packet. You can add the peas for the last 5 minutes of cooking time, if using.

Meanwhile, fry the pancetta, if using, in a little oil until crisp and brown.

Drain the pasta and leave in the saucepan. Add the tomato sauce, pancetta and mozzarella, season with salt and pepper and stir through.

Pour into an ovenproof dish and sprinkle with the Parmesan cheese. Cook in the preheated oven for 20–25 minutes, until the top is brown and bubbling.

I make this dish on a Monday after the roast that we regularly have on a Sunday. Usually I have leftover meat and it's so quick and easy, and Billie loves it – so it's a winner all round!

Special fried rice

SERVES 2

2 tablespoons vegetable oil

1 tablespoon sesame oil

1 garlic clove, finely chopped

4 spring onions, chopped

450 g (14½ oz) pre-cooked rice

100 g (3½ oz) leftover chicken or pork, chopped

2 eggs, beaten

50 g (2 oz) frozen peas, defrosted

soy sauce, to season

Heat the oils in a wok or large frying pan over a medium heat until smoking hot. Add the garlic and spring onions and fry very briefly before tipping in the rice and the meat. Cook for about 5 minutes, stirring all the time.

Add the eggs, peas and a good splash of soy sauce to season. Stir-fry until the eggs are set.

This was something Victoria and I made as students… except that I was never a student, she was – I was already working as an actress but I totally embraced her student lifestyle, including drinking in the student union bar! Whenever we couldn't be bothered to cook a big meal, this is what we made.

Tortilla

SERVES 4

3 tablespoons olive oil

2 garlic cloves, crushed slightly

400 g (13 oz) waxy potatoes, peeled and thinly sliced

1 large onion, thinly sliced

1 red pepper, quartered, deseeded and sliced in 2.5 cm (1 inch) lengths

8 large eggs

salt and pepper

Heat the olive oil in a 25 cm (10 inch) wide non-stick pan over a medium-low heat and gently cook the garlic for 5 minutes to infuse the oil with the flavour. Discard the garlic.

Add the potatoes, onion and pepper, turning through the oil to coat, and then cook gently until soft – this will take about 15–20 minutes. You may have to do this in batches. Once soft, drain off most of the oil, leaving the veg in the pan.

Beat the eggs in a bowl and season with salt and pepper. Pour into the pan over the other ingredients.

Cover the pan with a lid or aluminium foil and cook over a gentle heat until the eggs are set. You can finish this off under a hot grill if you wish to speed up the cooking.

Leave it to cool in the pan for at least 15 minutes then turn out on to a plate or board. Serve cut into wedges.

This is a dish that I have had many times at The Ivy in London. I remember first going there when I was about 26. I was with Angela, my best friend, and we were so over-excited that we had managed to get a table. I remember our dinner arriving and us wanting to take photos of each other and the food, only to be pounced upon by the waiter because no cameras are allowed in there. We drank champagne and spotted a few celebs, but mainly just ate fantastic food and laughed with each other all night. I had been told I had to have the iced berries and I thought they were beautiful. They are a great pudding if people come over unexpectedly because I always have bags of frozen berries in my freezer and I always have white chocolate. Super easy!

Iced berries with white chocolate sauce

SERVES 4

about 450 g (14½ oz) frozen berries (e.g. raspberries, blackberries, redcurrants, blackcurrants, blueberries)

150 g (5 oz) white chocolate

150 ml (¼ pint) double cream

Take the berries out of the freezer and arrange them on a serving plate 10 minutes before you are ready to serve.

Break up the white chocolate into small pieces and put them in a bowl. Put the cream in a saucepan and bring to a simmer. Pour over the chocolate and mix together until the chocolate has melted.

Immediately pour the white chocolate sauce over the berries and eat straight away!

This is a quick pudding that my godmother, Nina, used to make for last-minute dinner parties. I think it was a dish she picked up in America. She lived in Connecticut for a few years, and while she was over there my mum visited her quite often. We also went out for Thanksgiving, a magical time, and so began my own love affair with the United States!

Baked peaches with blueberries & mascarpone

SERVES 4

4 ripe peaches, halved and stoned

125 g (4 oz) blueberries

4 tablespoons caster sugar

250 g (8 oz) mascarpone

6 amaretti biscuits, crushed

Preheat the oven to 200°C (400°F), gas mark 6. Place the peaches, cut side up, in an ovenproof dish.

Put the blueberries, sugar and 1 tablespoon water in a saucepan over a low heat and gently cook until the berries start to burst.

Whisk the mascarpone in a bowl to soften, and mix in the blueberries. Spoon the mascarpone mixture into the holes of the peaches and then top with the crushed amaretti biscuits.

Bake in the preheated oven for about 10 minutes.

THE WAY I COOK...

when I want to make

Something Special

I thought this chapter was going to be the easiest to write, but it turned out to be the hardest. With all the cooking I'd been doing in restaurants and all the exciting stuff I've learnt, I presented my sister with the list of dishes I wanted to include. A lot of them she oohed and aahed over, but a few she looked at me as if to say, 'Are you having a laugh?!' I think I had probably got a little over-excited at what I wanted to share with you, except the thing is... it wasn't really cooking I would do at home. So I decided to try and take elements and put them into dishes that would be pretty, maybe a little harder than everyday food, but that anyone could still do at home, with confidence. And, believe me, I am still only learning – I spend quite a bit of time in professional kitchens and these recipes are inspired by my time in them.

One of the places I have been lucky enough to work in is Roux at Parliament Square. Steve Groves, who won *MasterChef: The Professionals* and is now head chef there, has become a good friend of mine. I think his food is amazing, he is so clever and I love cooking with him. He made these pickled cucumber ribbons and I had to steal the idea from him because after making them in the restaurant they were all I wanted to eat at home for weeks!

Smoked salmon with pickled cucumber

SERVES 4

300 g (10 oz) piece of smoked salmon, cubed

a small bunch of fresh dill, leaves picked, to garnish

FOR THE PICKLED CUCUMBER

125 ml (4 fl oz) rice vinegar

50 g (2 oz) caster sugar

1 teaspoon coriander seeds

2 dried bird's eye chillies

6 white peppercorns

2 cucumbers

2 tablespoons fine sea salt

To make the pickled cucumbers, combine the vinegar, sugar and spices in a saucepan and heat gently until the sugar has dissolved. Remove from the heat and leave to cool.

Peel the cucumbers, cut them in half lengthways and scoop out the seeds with a teaspoon and discard. Rub the cucumber halves with salt and set aside for 10 minutes. Rinse under cold water and pat dry.

Using a potato peeler, peel the cucumber into long ribbons and place in a large glass storage jar. Pour the spiced vinegar over the cucumber ribbons to cover and then seal the jar and place in the fridge for 3–4 hours or overnight.

Remove the cucumber ribbons from the vinegar and arrange on serving plates. Top with the cubed salmon and garnish with dill to finish.

I remember being taken out for a celebratory family dinner for passing my 11-plus. My mum and dad took me to a really old-fashioned Italian restaurant in Kingston and I ordered spaghetti alle vongole because I liked the name! I remember them looking at me, with slight surprise, and this huge bowl of steaming clams and spaghetti arrived. I thought it looked beautiful, wanted to keep all the shells and ate the whole bowl! Clams are similar to mussels, in that people often steer clear of cooking them at home in the mistaken belief that they will be tricky.

Spaghetti alle vongole

SERVES 4

1.5 kg (3 lb) clams (the small ones have the most flavour)

300 g (10 oz) spaghetti

olive oil

a knob of butter

3 garlic cloves, sliced

2 red chillies, chopped

250 ml (8 fl oz) white wine

a good handful of freshly chopped flat-leaf parsley

salt and pepper

Give the clams a good scrub and leave to soak for about 10 minutes in a large bowl of cold water. Empty the water and rinse again, to prevent your dish being gritty.

Meanwhile, put a large saucepan of water on to boil to cook the spaghetti, adding a good pinch of salt and a glug of olive oil.

Make sure you have everything ready as this all happens rather quickly. Melt the butter with a little olive oil in a large lidded saucepan over a medium heat. Add the garlic and fry gently. As the garlic starts to colour add the chillies and fry for a few seconds, then drop in the clams and wine. Put on the pan lid – this will steam the clams open (discard any that stay shut). Leave to cook for about 2–3 minutes so that the alcohol burns off and the liquid reduces a little.

Drain the spaghetti, saving about half a cup of the cooking water. Pour the spaghetti and the remaining water into the clams with the parsley and give it a good mix. Season with some salt and pepper. You can also add another little knob of butter or drizzle of olive oil to help the sauce stick to the pasta. Serve immediately.

Before I started working in restaurants I used to think the word 'confit' was terribly scary and something that I wouldn't be able to do. Actually it's very easy – you just salt the duck legs overnight and then cook them in duck fat... honestly, it's delicious! Also, they can keep in the fridge under the fat for a week. These duck legs can be used for the cassoulet recipe on page 28.

Confit duck

SERVES 6

150 g (5 oz) sea salt flakes

6 duck legs

a large bunch of fresh thyme

1 tablespoon white peppercorns

FOR THE CONFIT

1.25 kg (2½ lb) duck fat

1 garlic bulb, cloves separated

a bunch of fresh rosemary

a bunch of fresh thyme

4 fresh bay leaves

100 ml (3½ fl oz) white wine

1 tablespoon peppercorns

2 star anise

1 cinnamon stick

Rub the salt into the duck legs and place them in a large plastic container. Scoop up any excess salt and place in a pestle and mortar with the thyme and peppercorns. Pound gently to bruise the thyme and lightly crush the peppercorns, then sprinkle the mixture over the duck legs. Seal with a tight lid and refrigerate for 24 hours.

Preheat the oven to 140°C (275°F), gas mark 1. Remove the duck from the container and brush off any excess thyme and salt. Rinse under cold running water and pat dry.

Melt the duck fat in a large casserole. Gently bruise the garlic and herbs in a pestle and mortar and then add them to the casserole along with the wine, spices and salted duck legs. Find a saucepan lid slightly smaller than the casserole and lay this on top of the duck; this will prevent the duck from poking out of the fat. Set over a medium heat, bring to simmering point and then cover with a lid and transfer to the preheated oven. Cook for 2 hours – when it is ready the meat should pull away easily from the bone. Leave to cool for 1 hour. Remove the duck legs and divide between a couple of large glass storage jars. Pour the fat over the duck, ensuring the meat is completely covered. Refrigerate until you're ready to use.

To cook the duck legs: preheat the oven to 200°C (400°F), gas mark 6. Remove the duck legs from the jars and brush off any excess fat with a piece of kitchen paper (keep the fat as it can be used for making wonderful roast potatoes). Lay the duck legs skin side up in a roasting tray and cook for 20–25 minutes until the skin is crisp and golden.

Unless you have tasted proper, homemade gnocchi I would understand if the word that sprang to mind was 'meh'! Don't give up on gnocchi until you have tried making it yourself. It's really not difficult, and the sense of achievement is huge.

Gnocchi & Gorgonzola sauce

SERVES 4–6

200 ml (7 fl oz) double cream

200 g (7 oz) Gorgonzola cheese, crumbled (use the rind only in the sauce)

400 g (13 oz) floury potatoes, peeled and chopped

125 g (4 oz) plain flour, plus extra for dusting

1 egg yolk

1 tablespoon olive oil

butter, for frying

grated Parmesan cheese, to top

salt and pepper

Note: Preheat your grill while you are frying the gnocchi in butter. That way it will be nice and hot, ready for grilling when the sauce has heated through.

To make the sauce, place the cream in a small heavy-based pan and bring to the boil. Season liberally with ground black pepper and the rind from the Gorgonzola and cook for 5 minutes until reduced by one-third and thickened.

Put the potatoes in a pan, cover with water, add a pinch of salt and bring to the boil over a medium heat. Cook for about 10–12 minutes until soft. Drain and return to the pan. Place the pan over the heat and shake the potatoes to remove as much moisture as possible. Mash the potatoes well and season with salt but no pepper. Transfer to a bowl, add two-thirds of the flour and mix well. Add the egg yolk and mix.

Turn the mixture out on to a floured surface. Start to knead the potato and the flour together, adding a little more flour if it sticks to your hands (the potato must still be hot for this to work). Divide the dough into 4 and roll each portion into a large sausage about 3 cm (1½ inches) in diameter. Cut the potato into 3 cm (1½ inch) long pieces.

Pick up a piece of the dough and use the thumb of your right hand to press it against the back of a fork, rolling it off the end. Repeat the process with the rest of the dough.

Bring a pan of salted water and the olive oil to a boil and drop in the gnocchi. Leave to cook for a few minutes – they will float to the top. Cook for another 2 minutes.

Transfer the gnocchi to a frying pan with a knob of butter, and brown a little. Add the cheese sauce to the pan and heat through. Pour into an ovenproof dish and top with Parmesan and the crumbled Gorgonzola. Season with pepper and then heat under a hot grill until bubbling and well coloured.

I have spent many an afternoon making pasta and perfecting ravioli! This is a delicate dish, the crab so light and the beurre blanc fresh and delicious. Making your own pasta may seem a bit daunting at first (believe me, the first time I was asked to do it I didn't even know which way up the pasta machine was meant to go!). But actually it is quite easy, and really very satisfying. Once you have mastered this you can put herbs through your pasta and make all sorts of different shapes and sizes.

Crab ravioli with chive beurre blanc

SERVES 4

200 g (7 oz) fresh white crabmeat

50 g (2 oz) fresh brown crabmeat

2 spring onions, finely chopped

1 quantity Fresh Pasta Dough (see page 10)

salt and pepper

FOR THE SAUCE

1 shallot, finely chopped

5 black peppercorns

150 ml (¼ pint) dry white wine

150 ml (¼ pint) fish stock

2 teaspoons white wine vinegar

175 g (6 oz) cold unsalted butter, cut into cubes

a small bunch of fresh chives, finely chopped

For the filling, combine the crabmeats and spring onions in a bowl and season to taste. Cover and set aside until needed.

Make the pasta following the instructions on page 10 and roll it to the second thinnest setting. Lay the sheets on a well-floured surface. Place teaspoons of the mixture at 5 cm (2 inch) intervals along one side of the pasta, leaving a 1 cm (½ inch) gap between the filling and the edge of the sheet. Brush around the filling with a little water and then fold the pasta sheet over the filling and press down to seal, making sure you don't trap any pockets of air inside the pasta.

Using a ravioli wheel or sharp knife, cut around the filling to make a circle or square, then discard any trimmings. Lay the ravioli on a floured tray, dust with more flour and then cover with cling film or a clean tea towel while you make the sauce.

Tip the shallot, peppercorns, wine, fish stock and vinegar in a medium pan and bring to the boil. Boil for 5 minutes or until the liquid has reduced by two-thirds. Strain the liquid into a clean pan and bring to a simmer. Gradually whisk in the butter, until fully incorporated and the sauce is thick and glossy – make sure you don't add the butter too quickly as this can cause the sauce to split. Season to taste with a pinch of salt and stir through the chives just before serving.

Bring a large pan of salted water to the boil. Drop the ravioli in and cook for 2 minutes or until al dente. Drain, divide between 4 serving bowls and spoon over the sauce.

This rolled pork is a real showstopper and the stuffing is beautiful. Don't worry if the pork falls apart the first time; just roll the 'cracker' tighter next time!

Pork loin with lemon, garlic & parsley

SERVES 6–8

2.5 kg (5 lb) boned rolled loin of pork

50 g (2 oz) unsalted butter, plus 25 g (1 oz) extra, cold and cubed

10 garlic cloves, finely chopped

finely grated zest of 2 lemons

100 g (3½ oz) fresh white breadcrumbs

50 g (2 oz) fresh flat-leaf parsley, leaves finely chopped

salt and pepper

Preheat the oven to 220°C (425°F), gas mark 7. Using a sharp knife, carefully remove the skin from the pork, leaving on a layer of fat. Set aside.

Melt the butter in a large frying pan over a medium heat and then add the garlic and fry gently for 5 minutes until softened. Remove the pan from the heat and stir in the lemon zest, breadcrumbs and parsley. Season to taste.

Lay out 3 large sheets of foil, making sure they are at least 30 cm (12 inches) longer than the pork, then lay them on top of each other. Season the pork all over with plenty of salt and pepper and then lay it fat side down on the foil.

Sprinkle the breadcrumb mix over the pork in an even layer and press down firmly. Using the foil, wrap the pork up into a tight roll, twisting the ends of the foil to secure (you should end up with something that looks like a giant foil cracker).

Place a heavy-based roasting tin on top of the hob and set it over a high heat. Add the foil parcel to the roasting tin and seal for 5 minutes, turning continually. Transfer to the preheated oven, roast for 30 minutes and then turn the temperature down to 200°C (400°F), gas mark 6 and roast for a further 1 hour, turning halfway through. Remove from the oven and rest in the foil for 30 minutes.

Cut the foil off one end of the parcel and drain the roasting juices into a saucepan. Set over a medium heat and whisk in the cold butter. Remove from the heat and set aside.

Leaving the foil on, carve the pork into thick slices and then remove the foil (this makes it much easier to carve and helps the pork to hold its shape). Serve with the sauce.

This was one of the first things I cooked after feeling a little more confident in the kitchen. Boning the leg was really easy and I enjoyed doing it, but you can ask your butcher to do it for you.

Chicken ballotine & parfait potatoes

SERVES 4

2 chicken breasts, diced

100 ml (3½ fl oz) double cream

1 egg white

a small bunch of fresh tarragon, leaves finely chopped

500 ml (17 fl oz) chicken stock

2 garlic cloves, lightly crushed

2 thyme sprigs

4 large chicken thighs, boned

vegetable oil, for deep-frying

50 g (2 oz) cold unsalted butter, cubed

salt and white pepper

FOR THE POTATOES

400 g (13 oz) Charlotte potatoes, peeled and cut into wedges

50 g (2 oz) unsalted butter, softened

150 g (5 oz) chicken or duck liver parfait

Tip the diced chicken into a food processor and pulse until smooth. Add the cream and egg white and pulse again. Tip the mixture into a bowl, stir in the tarragon and season. Transfer to a piping bag then chill for 1 hour.

While the mousse chills, heat the stock, garlic and thyme in a small pan over a medium heat until reduced by two-thirds.

Lay each chicken thigh between 2 sheets of cling film and flatten with a rolling pin. Lay out a large sheet of cling film and lay a chicken thigh, skin side down, in the middle of the long edge of the film. Season the meat then pipe a quarter of the chicken mousse along the centre of the meat. Roll the chicken up tightly in the cling film and tie the ends to seal. Repeat with the remaining thighs and mousse.

Bring a large saucepan of water to the boil, add the chicken parcels, then cover and remove from the heat. Leave the chicken to poach gently for 20 minutes and then remove from the pan and leave to cool slightly. Remove the chicken from the cling film and pat dry with kitchen paper.

Meanwhile, bring a large pan of salted water to the boil, add the potatoes and cook until tender. Drain, return the potatoes to the warm pan and leave to steam for a couple of minutes. Combine the butter and liver parfait in a bowl then stir through the potatoes and season. Cover and keep warm.

Heat the oil for deep-frying to 170°C (325°F). Fry the chicken thighs in batches for 2–3 minutes until the skin is crisp and golden, then drain on kitchen paper. Leave to rest for a couple of minutes before carving into thick slices. Remove the thyme and garlic from the sauce and whisk in the cold butter. Serve the chicken with the sauce and potatoes.

This is such a lovely starter. Yes, I admit, it's 'cheffy', but nothing that can't be achieved at home. I have worked at a few of the *MasterChef* pop-up restaurants now and had to boil many an egg and peel them before deep-frying them. The thing is to be gentle and treat the eggs with care. They are worth a little bit of fuss, I promise!

Deep-fried egg with pancetta & endive salad

SERVES 4

4 large eggs, plus 2 beaten eggs

100 g (3½ oz) plain flour

100 g (3½ oz) Japanese panko breadcrumbs

6 smoked pancetta slices, cut in half

vegetable oil, for deep-frying

FOR THE SALAD

1 shallot, finely diced

100 ml (3½ fl oz) olive oil

50 ml (2 fl oz) white wine vinegar

1 teaspoon Dijon mustard

1 tablespoon freshly chopped tarragon

1 head of curly endive, green outer leaves discarded

1 Granny Smith apple, cored and cut into matchsticks

salt and pepper

Preheat the oven to 160°C (325°F), gas mark 3.

Boil the 4 eggs in a large saucepan of water for 5 minutes and then immediately plunge them into a bowl of iced water to stop them from cooking further. Carefully peel the eggs.

Put the flour, beaten eggs and breadcrumbs in 3 separate shallow bowls. Coat the boiled eggs in flour, dip in the beaten egg and finally roll in the breadcrumbs to coat. Transfer to the fridge for 15 minutes and then dip each egg in the beaten egg and roll in the breadcrumbs to give them a second coating.

Meanwhile, divide the pancetta between two non-stick baking trays, transfer to the oven and cook for 20 minutes until crisp. Drain on kitchen paper and set aside.

Heat the oil to 180°C (350°F) ready for deep-frying. Carefully lower the eggs into the hot oil and fry for 2–3 minutes until golden brown and crisp. Remove from the oil and drain on kitchen paper.

For the salad, combine the shallot, oil, vinegar, mustard and tarragon in a bowl and season to taste. Separate the yellow endive leaves and drop them into a bowl of iced water to crisp. Drain the leaves on kitchen paper and then toss with the apple and some of the shallot vinaigrette. Divide the salad between serving plates and finish with crispy pancetta. Serve with a crispy egg and a drizzle more of the vinaigrette.

Making your own pasta may seem a bit daunting at first (believe me, the first time I was asked to do it I didn't even know which way up the pasta machine was meant to go!). But actually it is quite easy.

My mum used to make this for her many dinner parties. It's retro and 80s but, you know what, sometimes things shouldn't be messed with, and I think rack of lamb is one of those things. The onion sauce is delicious – I remember the sweet smell of the onions cooking in my mum's kitchen, slowly bubbling away. It's an elegant and simple dish and one of my dinner party favourites.

Herb-crusted rack of lamb with white onion purée

SERVES 4

2 racks of lamb, trimmed

olive oil, for drizzling

100 g (3½ oz) dried white breadcrumbs

1 garlic clove, crushed

a small bunch of fresh flat-leaf parsley

4 rosemary sprigs, leaves picked

2 tablespoons finely grated Parmesan cheese

2 tablespoons Dijon mustard

salt and pepper

FOR THE PURÉE

50 g (2 oz) unsalted butter

3 onions, finely sliced

100 ml (3½ fl oz) full-fat milk

100 ml (3½ fl oz) double cream

ground white pepper

Preheat the oven to 200°C (400°F), gas mark 6.

For the onion purée, heat the butter in a frying pan over a low heat, add the onions and a pinch of salt and fry slowly for 20–25 minutes, until completely soft but not coloured. Add the milk and cream and cook for a further 10 minutes. Leave to cool slightly and then transfer to a food processor or blender and blitz until smooth and velvety. Season to taste with salt and white pepper and then return to a clean saucepan and reheat gently before serving.

Drizzle the lamb with olive oil and season with salt and pepper. Heat a large frying pan over a high heat, add the lamb racks and sear for 3–4 minutes until golden brown all over. Remove from the pan and set aside to cool.

Put the breadcrumbs, garlic, parsley, rosemary and Parmesan in a food processor or blender and blitz until the mixture turns to the consistency of wet sand – if the mixture is too dry, add a little olive oil and blitz again. Season to taste and then transfer to a plate or shallow roasting tin.

Brush the meat with the mustard and then roll in the herb mixture. Lay the lamb on a baking tray and roast in the preheated oven for 8–10 minutes. Transfer to a warm plate to rest for 5 minutes and then carve into cutlets. Serve with the onion purée and some seasonal vegetables.

I have always found the idea of cooking osso bucco at home a little daunting, I don't know why. I think it might have something to do with the name! It is such a fabulous dish – the braised veal, the vegetables that help thicken the sauce and the delicious oozing marrowbone, which is yummy on crusty bread. Osso bucco is great served with creamy *pommes mousseline* and gremolata.

Osso bucco with gremolata

SERVES 4

60 ml (2 fl oz) olive oil

4 large veal shin slices, around 3 cm (1½ inches) thick, trimmed of any excess fat

plain flour, for dusting

a knob of unsalted butter

1 onion, finely chopped

1 carrot, finely chopped

2 celery sticks, finely chopped

2 garlic cloves, crushed

1 tablespoon tomato purée

1 bay leaf

1 rosemary sprig

2 thyme sprigs

250 ml (8 fl oz) white wine

350 ml (12 fl oz) fresh veal or chicken stock

salt and pepper

FOR THE GREMOLATA

finely grated zest of 1 lemon

1 garlic clove, finely chopped

2 tablespoons freshly chopped parsley

Note: Ask your butcher for the thickest part of the shin – this will give you more of the delicious bone marrow in the centre.

Preheat the oven to 150°C (300°F), gas mark 2.

Heat 2 tablespoons of the olive oil in a large heavy-based casserole. Place the veal shin slices in a plastic sandwich bag with a handful of flour and plenty of salt and pepper. Close the bag and shake to coat the meat. Remove the meat and add to the hot oil. Sear for 2 minutes on each side until golden brown, remove from the pan and set aside.

Add 2 more tablespoons of oil to the pan along with a knob of butter. When the butter is foaming, add the onion, carrot and celery and fry for 5 minutes until softened and starting to caramelise. Add the garlic, fry for a further 2 minutes and then add the tomato purée and herbs. Fry for 2 minutes and then add the wine. Bring to the boil and simmer for 5 minutes until reduced. Add the stock and return the veal to the pan, ensuring the meat is completely covered.

Transfer to the preheated oven and cook for 2 hours until the meat is tender. You may need to check the casserole occasionally – if the sauce is drying out, add a splash of stock or water to the pan.

To make the gremolata, combine the ingredients in a small bowl and season with a little salt and black pepper.

Serve the osso bucco with a sprinkle of gremolata.

I first had this at Smiths. It was on the top floor menu and when I had to make it my mouth would literally water, so much so that I would drop massive hints during service like, 'Mmm, they look so amazing…' Eventually, Michael, the head chef, took pity on me and made me one, though he actually said it was to shut me up!

Deep-fried ham hock with piccalilli dipping sauce

SERVES 4—6

1 smoked or unsmoked ham hock

1 smoked ham hock

a bouquet garni

1 shallot

1 carrot

6 peppercorns

a handful of freshly chopped parsley

2 teaspoons mustard

2–3 tablespoons plain flour

2 eggs, beaten

150 g (5 oz) dried breadcrumbs

4 tablespoons vegetable oil

2–3 tablespoons piccalilli

salt and pepper

Put the ham hocks in a large saucepan with the bouquet garni, shallot, carrot and peppercorns. Cover with water and bring to the boil. Cover with a circle of greaseproof paper and simmer for about 2–3 hours. Remove the meat, strain and reserve the liquid.

Take the skin and fat off the hocks but leave a little of the jelly. Shred the hock in a bowl and add the parsley, mustard, 75 ml (3½ fl oz) of the reserved cooking liquid and some salt and pepper.

Spread a layer of cling film over a baking tray and then press the mixture down on to half of the cling film (so half the tray has ham on it). Fold the other half of the cling film over the ham and set in the fridge for at least 2–3 hours.

When set, cut the ham into triangles – you should get about 12. Put the flour, eggs and breadcrumbs in 3 separate shallow bowls. Dip the ham triangles in flour, then egg and finally breadcrumbs and ensure that they are well coated.

Heat the vegetable oil in a frying pan and fry the ham until golden on both sides. Drain on kitchen paper.

To make the sauce, put the piccalilli in a bowl and blend it briefly with a hand-held blender until the sauce is a good dipping consistency. Serve the fried ham while still hot with little pots of the dipping sauce.

I first cooked venison on MasterChef and have since cooked with it many times at home. It is a delicious meat and the chocolate sauce in this recipe is incredible with it. This is a classic dish and very straightforward. Give it a go!

Venison, celeriac & apple purée, red wine & chocolate sauce

SERVES 4

600 g (1 lb 2 oz) venison loin, trimmed

olive oil

1 tablespoon juniper berries, crushed

2 thyme sprigs

2 garlic cloves, bruised

50 g (2 oz) unsalted butter

salt and pepper

1 quantity Red Wine and Chocolate Sauce (see page 12), to serve

FOR THE PURÉE

1 celeriac head, peeled and cubed

500 ml (17 fl oz) milk

500 ml (17 fl oz) water

2 Bramley apples, peeled, cored and diced

1 tablespoon caster sugar

25 g (1 oz) unsalted butter

white pepper

Preheat the oven to 180°C (350°F), gas mark 4. Make the sauce (see page 12) and keep warm until needed.

To make the purée, place the celeriac in a large saucepan with the milk and water. Bring to the boil and then simmer gently until the celeriac is soft. Strain the celeriac and reserve the cooking liquid. Meanwhile, put the apple and caster sugar into a saucepan with a splash of water and simmer gently until the apple is soft and beginning to break apart. Spoon the apple and celeriac into a food processor or blender with a ladleful of the celeriac cooking liquid. Blitz until smooth, adding a little more liquid if needed. Add the butter and season to taste with salt and white pepper. Pour into a saucepan and reheat gently before serving.

Rub the venison loin with olive oil and season with plenty of salt and pepper. Crush the juniper berries in a pestle and mortar and rub over the meat. Heat a large ovenproof frying pan over a high heat, add the venison and sear on all sides for 5 minutes until golden brown. Add the thyme, garlic and butter to the pan and baste the venison for 2 minutes. Cover the meat with foil and then transfer the pan to the preheated oven for 8 minutes. Remove the meat from the pan and leave to rest on a warm plate for 10 minutes.

Carve the venison into thick slices and serve with the celeriac and apple purée, the red wine and chocolate sauce and some simple green vegetables such as kale or Savoy cabbage.

When I was working at Smiths, I always wanted to eat this! I love that you got a great plate of beef sliced at your table with all the sauces you wanted. Whenever I ate there, though, I was never with anyone who wanted to share this with me… I am still dreaming!

Chateaubriand with slow-roasted onions & fondant potato

SERVES 4

4 small onions, unpeeled

olive oil, for drizzling

1 kg (2 lb) piece of centre-cut beef fillet, trimmed

1 garlic bulb, cut in half through the middle

200 ml (7 fl oz) red wine

50 g (2 oz) cold unsalted butter, cubed

salt and pepper

FOR THE FONDANT POTATOES

600 g (1 lb 2 oz) waxy potatoes, such as Charlotte

100 g (3½ oz) unsalted butter

500 ml (17 fl oz) chicken stock

3 garlic cloves, bashed

2 thyme sprigs

Preheat the oven to 190°C (375°), gas mark 5. Put the onions in a small roasting tin, drizzle with oil and sprinkle with salt. Roast for 30 minutes, or until soft and sticky (you can check that the onions are cooked by pushing a skewer into the flesh; it should be soft). Remove from the oven and keep warm.

To make the potatoes. Peel them and trim the ends to make a barrel shape. Heat a little oil in a large, deep frying pan and add the butter. Once the butter is foaming, add the potatoes, standing them on their ends. Fry gently for 5–6 minutes or until the undersides are golden. Turn the potatoes over and then add the stock, garlic and thyme. Bring the stock to the boil, then simmer gently for 20–25 minutes until the potatoes are cooked through and most of the liquid has evaporated. Remove from the heat and keep warm.

Once the onions are cooked, turn the oven up to 200°C (400°F), gas mark 6. Preheat a large pan over a high heat until smoking. Rub the beef with oil and season generously. Put it in the frying pan with the garlic bulb, cut side down. Sear the beef for 5 minutes until golden all over, then transfer to a roasting tin along with the garlic.

Roast the beef for 15–20 minutes, depending on how you like it cooked; transfer to a warm plate and rest for 15 minutes. Remove the garlic and set the roasting pan over a high heat. Deglaze the tin with the wine and boil until reduced by half. Squeeze the garlic flesh into the pan then whisk in the butter. Season to taste. Carve the beef into thick slices and serve with the onions, potatoes and a good drizzle of the sauce.

I absolutely LOVE this dish. 'Consommé' was another word that used to scare me and I would never have attempted this, but it really is only a clear soup. Yes, a little extra work goes into it, but we are in the Something Special chapter and I don't think you would be here unless you, like me, thought that you could do this and, like me, love cooking...

Cod fillet with tomato consommé

SERVES 4

4 ripe tomatoes (I use a mixture of red, orange and yellow), peeled, deseeded and diced

½ cucumber, peeled, deseeded and diced

a small bunch of fresh chives, finely chopped

4 centre-cut pieces of cod fillet, skin on, weighing about 150 g (5 oz) each

olive oil, for brushing

salt and pepper

FOR THE CONSOMMÉ

1 kg (2 lb) very ripe tomatoes, roughly chopped

½ cucumber, roughly chopped

a small bunch of fresh basil, stalks included

1 red chilli, deseeded and roughly chopped

1 tablespoon freshly grated horseradish

a pinch of caster sugar

sherry vinegar, to taste

Note: The tomatoes are the real heroes of this dish – use the very best and ripest you can find.

First make the consommé. Tip all the ingredients plus a little salt into a food processor or blender and blitz until smooth. Taste the pulp to check for seasoning and adjust with a little more salt and sherry vinegar.

Either suspend a muslin jelly bag over a large saucepan or bowl, or line a large sieve with a muslin cloth, then carefully pour in the blended pulp. Leave the mixture to drip slowly through the muslin for 3–4 hours or in a cool place overnight. Do not be tempted to squeeze the muslin as this will turn the consommé cloudy. Once the liquid has stopped dripping through, discard the pulp – you should be left with a beautifully clear liquid that tastes incredible.

To prepare the rest of the recipe, combine the diced tomatoes and cucumber with a good pinch of chives and season with a pinch of salt. Pile a small mound of the mixture in the centre of each serving bowl.

Heat a large non-stick frying pan over a medium to high heat. Brush the cod skin with oil and season with salt and pepper. Lay the fish in the pan skin side down and fry for 5 minutes until the fish has turned white two-thirds of the way through the flesh and the skin is crisp and golden. Turn the fish over, remove the pan from the heat and leave for 2 minutes – the residual heat in the pan will finish cooking the fish.

Lay a piece of cod on top of the tomato and cucumber salad and carefully pour the consommé around the outside. Serve at room temperature.

I first met Steve Groves, at the *MasterChef* pop-up restaurant. I was slightly in awe after watching him win *MasterChef: The Professionals,* and remember shaking his hand and him being quite gruff with me. I decided the best thing to do was just get my head down and work. I was filleting fish and Steve came up and showed me an easier way to clean the blood line. I'm not sure how we became mates but I think he saw how very much I wanted to learn and decided to give me a break. Since then I have cooked quite a lot with him. I thought his fish with a jacket potato crust was inspired. I asked my voice of reason, Victoria, if she would ever attempt this and she said yes! I know it's proper cheffy, but it's great, and there should be enough crust to freeze for a later date.

Halibut with baked potato crust

SERVES 4

4 halibut fillets, weighing about 300 g (10 oz) each

FOR THE BAKED POTATO POWDER

4 large red-skinned potatoes

1 tablespoon fresh chervil or a few slices of Preserved Lemons (see page 106)

25 g (1 oz) unsalted butter

salt and pepper

FOR THE CRUST

90 g (3½ oz) soft, unsalted butter

25 g (1 oz) breadcrumbs

65 g (2½ oz) baked potato powder (see above)

50 g (2 oz) Parmesan cheese, finely grated

½ egg, beaten

½ tablespoon fresh thyme leaves

Preheat the oven to 200°C (400°F), gas mark 6.

Wash and scrub some red-skinned potatoes until completely clean. Bake them on a baking tray covered in salt for about 1–1½ hours until cooked.

Scoop out the insides of the potatoes into a bowl and stir through a tablespoon of fresh chervil or a few slices of preserved lemons. Add the butter, season with salt and pepper and keep warm until the fish is cooked.

Put the potato skins back in the oven until golden brown. Turn the oven down to 120°C (250°F), gas mark ½ and let them dry out completely, about 1–1½ hours.

Put the dried-out skins in a food processor or blender and blitz until they are powder.

Mix all the crust ingredients together, then roll out between 2 pieces of greaseproof paper. Transfer to the fridge until needed. Once chilled, cut the crust to fit the halibut fillets and set aside.

Pan-fry the halibut in a hot frying pan for about 2-3 minutes on each side. Place the crust on top of each fillet, then cook under a hot grill until crisp. Serve with the mashed potato and a green vegetable, such as samphire.

A few months after I won MasterChef, I was asked if I wanted to be involved in the *MasterChef* pop-up restaurant with Dhruv, Tim Kinnaird and Alex Rushmer (*MasterChef* finalists), as well as a few other past *MasterChef* contestants. I jumped at the chance. The head chef of the restaurant that we took over was a lovely, and bonkers (aren't they all?!), Spanish guy called Javi. I was on Alex's ceviche for most of the time and I have fond memories of Javi hollering 'LEEZA, CEVICHEEE' at the top of his voice! It was great fun and adrenaline-pumping, with beautiful food being cooked, and this is where the inspiration for this dish comes from. The thing I love about this recipe is that it's so colourful, with the grapefruit, onions, coriander and red chilli. And all you have to do is tower it rather prettily on to a plate to serve.

Sea bass ceviche

SERVES 4–6

475 g (15 oz) well-chilled sea bass fillets

1 lime, juice only

pink Florida grapefruit, segmented, half used for juice the other half chopped

1 red chilli, very finely sliced

4 spring onions, very finely sliced

a handful of freshly chopped coriander

salt and pepper

Slice the very cold fish fillets as finely as you can (this will be easiest with a very sharp knife), and place them in a bowl.

Add the lime juice, grapefruit juice and chopped segments, chilli, spring onions, coriander and season with salt and freshly ground black pepper. Combine with your fingers so that when you arrange on the plate there will be a little bit of everything. Serve immediately.

My best friend Angela cooked this dish when she first moved into her new flat in West Hampstead in London. We were both girls about town then, and really saw eating as a bit of a necessity so that we could go out and drink! But this was a proper grown-up recipe for us. That was 14 years ago, and we still cook it today…

Steamed lemon sole with tapenade & shaved fennel salad

SERVES 4

8 lemon sole fillets

salt and pepper

FOR THE TAPENADE

200 g (7 oz) pitted Kalamata olives

1 garlic clove, crushed

2 tablespoons capers

4 anchovy fillets, drained

a small bunch of fresh parsley, leaves chopped

a small bunch of fresh basil, leaves chopped

grated zest and juice of 1 lemon

3 tablespoons extra virgin olive oil

½ teaspoon cayenne pepper

FOR THE SALAD

2 fennel bulbs

grated zest and juice of 1 lemon

a bunch of radishes, trimmed

2 celery sticks, peeled

extra virgin olive oil

a small bunch of fresh chives, finely chopped

For the tapenade, combine all of the ingredients in a food processor or blender and blitz to a paste. Season to taste and set aside.

For the salad, finely shave the fennel on a mandoline and immediately toss in the lemon juice to prevent it from discolouring. Shave the radishes and celery on the mandoline and add to the fennel with the lemon zest, a good drizzle of olive oil and the chives. Season to taste.

Roll the lemon sole fillets into neat parcels, secure each with a cocktail stick and season with salt and pepper. Line a steamer with greaseproof paper, add the sole and steam for 4 minutes or until just cooked through.

Serve the sole with the tapenade and fennel salad.

This is inspired by the wonderful Tom Kitchin. He really is one of my favourite chefs; his food is truly awesome. I went to have lunch at The Kitchin in Edinburgh, and we had the tasting menu. Tom talked us through the stories behind the dishes and I can honestly say that every course was amazing. He demoed these scallops at The Good Food Show in Glasgow, so I got to see first hand how he did it.

Scallops with julienne of ginger & carrots in vermouth

SERVES 4

400 ml (14 fl oz) fish stock

25 g (1 oz) butter

2 carrots, julienned

½ leek, julienned

1 celery stick, julienned

1 thumb-size piece of fresh ginger, julienned

50 ml (2 fl oz) vermouth

50 ml (2 fl oz) double cream

4 large scallops in their shells

1 pack of ready-rolled puff pastry

1 egg, beaten

salt and pepper

Put the fish stock in a saucepan over a high heat and boil to reduce until you have a syrup (it should be about 100 ml (3½ fl oz) of liquid).

Melt the butter in a frying pan over a medium-low heat and sweat down the vegetables and ginger. Season. Make sure you soften them but still keep a bit of texture to them. Set aside.

Put the vermouth and cream in a saucepan over a high heat and boil to reduce to about 100 ml (3½ fl oz), then add the fish stock. Taste and season with salt and pepper.

Clean the scallops. Take them out of their shells and really scrub the shells too. Cut off the roes and discard.

On a baking tray make 4 'nests' out of foil (these are to place the scallops on so that they stay upright).

Place the shells on top of the foil nests, evenly spoon in the julienned veg, then top with the scallop and the cream sauce. Refrigerate for 30 minutes.

Cut the puff pastry sheet into 4 and indent the scallop shells so you have that lovely shape on the pastry. Place the pastry over the shells and press down, as if you are tucking them in. Glaze with egg wash and rest again in the fridge for 30 minutes. Meanwhile, preheat the oven to 190°C (375°F), gas mark 5. Cook the scallops in the preheated oven for 15 minutes until golden and risen.

This is another recipe I learnt while at Roux at Parliament Square. If you have never been, I recommend going! Steve is one of the most inspiring chefs I have ever worked with; his food is so clever and the flavours always delicate and subtle. Every time I get the chance to work with him I come away full of admiration and ideas.

Chocolate brownie with peanut butter parfait

SERVES 6–8

FOR THE BROWNIE

350 g (11½ oz) dark chocolate

250 g (8 oz) butter

375 g (12 oz) caster sugar

5 eggs

65 g (2½ oz) flour, sifted

65 g (2½ oz) cocoa powder

1½ teaspoons baking powder

150 g (5 oz) white chocolate, chopped

FOR THE PEANUT PRALINE

75 g (3 oz) peanuts

50 g (2 oz) caster sugar

FOR THE PEANUT BUTTER PARFAIT

3 egg whites

75 g (3 oz) caster sugar

75 g (3 oz) smooth peanut butter

125 g (4 oz) peanut praline (see above)

190 g (6½ oz) double cream

Note: This recipe is suitable for freezing once cooked.

To make the praline, place the peanuts on a baking tray lined with greaseproof paper. Melt the sugar in a saucepan – make sure you don't stir it – until it just starts to colour. Pour the melted sugar evenly over the peanuts. Leave to set at room temperature and then break up into pieces, transfer to a food processor and blitz until it resembles crumbs.

To make the parfait, whisk together the egg whites and, when stiff, add the caster sugar and continue to whisk until stiff peaks form again. Beat together the peanut butter and praline and then fold this into the meringue. Lightly whip the cream and fold this into the mixture. Spoon into a cling film-lined baking tray and transfer to the freezer for 2 hours until firm.

Preheat the oven to 180°C (350°F), gas mark 4. Line a 25 x 20 x 5 cm (10 x 8 x 2½ inch) baking tray with baking paper.

Melt the dark chocolate and butter over a bain-marie.

Mix together the sugar and eggs with a hand-held electric whisk or in a food processor until smooth. Add the melted chocolate and butter and stir to mix.

Fold in the sifted flour, cocoa and baking powder and then mix in the white chocolate. Spread the mixture on to a lined baking tray and cook in the preheated oven for 45 minutes. Leave to cool on a wire rack for 30 minutes. Serve the brownie cut into triangles with a quenelle of parfait on top.

The word soufflé is enough to have even the most seasoned cook running for the hills! I was so green when I started *MasterChef* that I had no idea about this and attempted one in the semi-finals – luckily, it worked! I remember announcing I was 'going to do a soufflé', only to be met with a sharp intake of breath and a mumble of, 'That's brave.' The thing with soufflés is that there are lots of elements that all have to work, plus little things that can trip you up along the way – so don't despair if it doesn't work, just keep practising.

Chocolate soufflés

SERVES 6—8

90 g (3½ oz) unsalted butter, plus 25 g (1 oz), melted, for brushing

90 g (3½ oz) good-quality dark chocolate, melted, plus a little extra, grated, for dusting

450 ml (¾ pint) milk

1 vanilla pod

60 g (2¼ oz) plain flour

25 g (1 oz) cocoa powder

6 eggs, separated, plus 2 egg yolks

4 tablespoons caster sugar, plus extra for lining the moulds

double cream, to serve

Preheat the oven to 190°C (375°F), gas mark 5. Brush 6–8 150 ml (¼ pint) ramekin dishes with melted butter and then dust with the finely grated dark chocolate. Transfer the dishes to the fridge while you prepare the soufflés.

Put the milk in a saucepan. Split the vanilla pod lengthways, scrape the seeds into the milk and drop the pod in too. Bring the milk to a boil.

Beat the butter in a bowl until smooth and then sift in the flour and cocoa. Pour over the warm milk and beat in the egg yolks. Return the mixture to the pan and heat over a medium heat, stirring, until thickened. Remove from the heat and beat in the melted chocolate. Cover with a circle of greaseproof paper or some cling film while you whisk the egg whites.

Whisk the egg whites until fluffy. Add the sugar a little at a time and whisk until stiff peaks form. Stir 2 tablespoons of the egg whites into the chocolate and then carefully fold in the rest, taking care not to knock out the air.

Fill the ramekin dishes up to the top and then bang them down on to the worktop to knock out any air bubbles. Use a palette knife to flatten the top of each soufflé and then run your thumb along the inside of the rim – this helps to ensure that they don't catch or stick to the edges when they rise. Bake in the oven for 9–11 minutes. The soufflés should be well-risen. The top needs to be set but they should still wobble slightly when shaken. Serve with a jug of double cream.

I have a second cousin called Jane who lives in Canada. When she said she was coming over to London this summer, my whole family was very excited. My dad brought them all up to my house, and my sis and her family came over and I cooked a huge feast. I wanted to make a summer dessert that was light and fresh and a little different (I also hadn't left myself much time!). These meringues are super-easy and the cream and praline take no time at all, plus it can be done in stages. Suffice to say, Jane and her lovely husband Norm and our families swapped stories and photos and ate… like kings!!

Meringue discs with passion fruit cream & pistachio praline

SERVES 6

4 egg whites

a pinch of salt

200 g (7 oz) caster sugar

FOR THE PRALINE

100 g (3½ oz) pistachio nuts, chopped

125 g (4 oz) caster sugar

4 tablespoons water

FOR THE PASSION FRUIT CREAM

4–5 passion fruit

300 ml (½ pint) whipping cream

1 tablespoon icing sugar

Preheat the oven to 140°C (275°F), gas mark 1 and line a baking sheet with greaseproof paper.

Whisk the egg whites with the salt in a large clean bowl, either by hand or with a hand-held electric mixer, until very stiff and then gradually whisk in the sugar. Continue whisking until the mixture is glossy and quite stiff. Using a large spoon, scoop 6 discs of meringue on to the prepared baking tray. Cook in the oven for 45 minutes. Turn the oven off but leave the meringues inside for 30 minutes.

Meanwhile, make the praline. Spread some baking parchment on a baking tray or use a silicone sheet and scatter the pistachios evenly. Put the sugar and water in a small saucepan and bring to the boil. When the sugar is boiling and starting to turn golden, remove from the heat and leave for about 30 seconds before pouring over the nuts. Leave to set.

To make the cream, scoop the passion fruit flesh into a bowl. In a separate bowl, whisk the cream, by hand or using an electric whisk, until it holds its shape, but be careful not to over-whip (you want a syllabub-type texture). Lightly fold through the passion fruit and icing sugar.

To serve, put a meringue on a plate with a spoonful of the cream and a crumbling of the praline on top.

This is properly 'old school' and properly impressive. I think you can probably gauge that if I could step back into the 80s I would! This is a little bit of a cheat's version because I use a shop-bought sponge base, but it's still really delicious. Make sure you have enough room in your freezer to store it for an hour, or however long, before you are going to cook it. You may also be thinking, 'Baked ice cream? How?' But it really does work!

Baked Alaska

SERVES 4–6

1 soft sponge flan case, 18–20 cm (7–8 inch) in diameter

250 g (8 oz) strawberries, hulled and sliced

2 tablespoons elderflower cordial

500 g (1 lb) vanilla ice cream (not soft scoop)

4 egg whites

200 g (7 oz) caster sugar

Put the sponge flan case on a baking tray and arrange the strawberries over the sponge base. Pour over the elderflower cordial so that it soaks into the sponge.

Tip the ice cream into a bowl that will fit into the flan case when inverted and push down so that it will come out as a dome shape. Invert the bowl so that you now have a dome of ice cream sitting on top of the strawberries and cordial.

Transfer the baking tray to the freezer, uncovered, so that it stays as frozen as possible.

Whisk the egg whites in a clean dry bowl until it forms stiff peaks. Add the caster sugar a little at a time and continue to whisk until shiny and glossy peaks form.

Remove the sponge from the freezer and swirl the meringue on top. Return to the freezer for 1 hour or until you need to use it. You can make this in the morning and it will still be okay by the evening.

When you are ready to cook, preheat the oven to 200°C (400°F), gas mark 6.

Place in the preheated oven for about 5 minutes, just until the meringue starts to brown at the peaks. Serve immediately.

I love chocolate tart – I love chocolate! But I am fussy; the chocolate has to be soft and shiny and bitter, and the pastry has to be really crisp, so that you get that lovely rich smooth filling and a snap of sweet pastry. This tart is lovely served with cream, and if I want to make it a little more special, I like to dust a bit of honeycomb to finish, which I just blitz in a food processor and sprinkle over the top. It's a little bit 'cheffy', but really simple. This is a really rich tart and you don't need very much, just a sliver.

Chocolate tart

SERVES 10–12

flour, for dusting

1 quantity chilled Sweet Pastry (see page 214)

1 egg, beaten

390 ml (13½ fl oz) double cream

25 g (1 oz) liquid glucose

365 g (11½ oz) good-quality dark chocolate, cut into small pieces

85 g (3½ oz) unsalted butter, diced

75 g (3 oz) honeycomb, crushed to a powder

Preheat the oven to 200°C (400°F), gas mark 6.

Remove the pastry dough from the fridge and, leaving it between the 2 pieces of greaseproof paper, roll out the disc to a slightly larger circle than a 20 cm (8 inch) tart tin. Use the pastry to line the tin and then bake blind in the preheated oven for 12–15 minutes.

Remove the baking beans from the pastry and return the tart to the oven for a further 5–10 minutes.

Brush the pastry with beaten egg and dry either at room temperature or in the preheated oven for 2 minutes. Make sure the tart is properly cooled before adding the filling.

While the tart is cooling, pour the cream and the glucose into a saucepan over a medium heat and bring to a simmer.

Pour the cream on to the chocolate pieces in a bowl and whisk together until the chocolate has completely melted.

Whisk in the diced butter and then pour the mixture into the prepared pastry case. Transfer to the fridge to chill for at least 2 hours, but best overnight. Serve at room temperature topped with the honeycomb powder.

VARIATION:
You could add a dash of cognac to the chocolate mixture if you wanted to!

THE WAY I COOK...

when the Sun is Shining

I am at my happiest! The kitchen doors are open, Billie is bouncing on the trampoline or playing with her dolls in the paddling pool, and I am either sitting at the garden table writing a list of what ingredients to buy or cooking. I love making jugs of iced tea and summer jellies and picnic food, but also salads and marinades and having barbecues. I think what is lovely about this country is that we know that the hot weather never lasts, and that the countryside is truly beautiful when the sun shines, so we make the most of it. Supermarket shelves of barbecue food and picnic stuff is sold out in a matter of hours so it's nice to be able to make your own, to sit back in your garden and throw open your doors and embrace the so-short but so-amazing British summertime!

Steak and salad, mmmm... what's not to love? And the pickled walnuts add a lovely sharpness to the dish. Perfect for a summertime lunch.

Seared beef salad

SERVES 4

4 sirloin steaks, weighing about 100 g (3½ oz) each

75 ml (3 fl oz) olive oil, plus extra for rubbing

1 tablespoon red wine vinegar

1 teaspoon mustard powder

grated rind of 1 lemon

50 g (2 oz) rocket

50 g (2 oz) watercress

a handful of sliced pickled walnuts

salt and pepper

Rub the steaks with a little olive oil and season with salt and pepper.

Heat a frying or grill pan and add 1 tablespoon of the olive oil. When the pan is smoking hot, add the steaks and cook for about 2 minutes on each side. Leave to rest on a warm plate or board and reserve the juices.

In a jug, whisk together the remaining olive oil, red wine vinegar and mustard powder. Add the lemon rind and the meat juices, whisk again and season to taste.

Slice the steaks thinly on an angle and spoon over a little of the dressing so that the meat is coated.

Put the rocket and watercress in a serving bowl, season and spoon over the dressing. Toss until the leaves are coated. Mix through the pickled walnuts.

Place the steak on top of the leaves and serve immediately.

This is the first thing that John Torode taught me to cook after *MasterChef*. I was desperate to get some experience in kitchens and had asked John if I could possibly work at Smiths. I think he wasn't sure that I actually meant it. I kept on at him, and eventually he said yes. He made this look so effortless and I was secretly thinking that there was no way I'd be able to do it, but I did. The bisque tastes like velvet…

Bisque & rouille

SERVES 4–6

1 lobster

FOR THE BISQUE

50 ml (2 fl oz) vegetable oil

1 large onion, chopped

2 large carrots, chopped

2 celery stalks, chopped

3 over-ripe tomatoes, chopped

4 garlic cloves, crushed

75 g (3 oz) rice

2 lemongrass stalks

50 g (2 oz) galangal, chopped

4 whole star anise

100 ml (3½ fl oz) brandy

2 litres (3½ pints) water

25 ml (1 fl oz) fish sauce

a dash of oyster sauce, to serve

FOR THE ROUILLE

6 garlic cloves

2 egg yolks

250 ml (8 fl oz) extra virgin olive oil

a pinch of cayenne pepper

¼ teaspoon saffron threads

salt

Remove the meat from the body of the lobster and set aside for another use, together with the claws and tail (keep the shells).

Make the bisque: heat the oil in a saucepan over a medium heat, add the lobster shells and cook gently until they turn dark red. Add the chopped onion, carrots, celery and tomatoes and cook gently for 5 minutes until the vegetables soften. Add the garlic and the rice and cook for 5 minutes, then add the lemongrass, galangal and star anise.

Pour in the brandy, flambé and bring to the boil, scraping the base of the pan. Add 1.5 litres (2½ pints) of the water and the fish sauce, bring back to the boil, reduce the heat to a simmer and cook for 2 hours. Add the remaining water halfway through the cooking time. Remember to stir and scrape the base of the pan regularly so that the rice doesn't stick. By the end of the cooking time, the bisque should have reduced to the thickness of a sauce. Strain and keep warm if using immediately. Otherwise, leave to cool and keep in the fridge until ready to reheat.

To make the rouille, peel the garlic, smash it with a knife and sprinkle it with salt. Pound to a paste either in a pestle and mortar or on a board, pressing down with the side of a knife. Put the egg yolks in a bowl and whisk until pale. Add the garlic paste and mix together. Whisk in the olive oil slowly until it thickens. Add the cayenne pepper and saffron and stir through. Season to taste and serve with the bisque and a dash of oyster sauce.

I have made this salad on the top floor at Smiths and in Roux at Parliament Square. It was one of the first dishes I was given to do, so they obviously trusted me enough to know I wouldn't mess it up! It's very easy to prepare and it's all in the presentation – remember, we eat with our eyes.

Heritage varieties of beetroot, such as Candy Striped and Golden, add beautiful colours to this salad and are perfect for cooking with in the summer months, but if you can't get hold of them just substitute with the more common red beetroot.

Beetroot salad

SERVES 4

3 tablespoons rock salt or sea salt flakes

3 large red beetroot, washed but not peeled

2 teaspoons sherry vinegar

juice of ½ a lemon

2 tablespoons extra virgin olive oil

1 Candy Striped beetroot, peeled

1 Golden beetroot, peeled

2 Braeburn apples, cored and sliced into matchsticks

100 g (3½ oz) soft goat's cheese, crumbled

a small bunch of basil, leaves picked

2 tablespoons pine nuts, lightly toasted

sea salt and pepper

Preheat the oven to 200°C (400°F), gas mark 6.

Make three piles of salt in the bottom of a roasting tray and sit a red beetroot on top of each one. Cover the tray with foil and bake in the preheated oven for 45 minutes or until completely cooked through and soft. When cool enough to handle, peel the beetroot (you may want to wear rubber gloves to avoid staining your fingers).

Whisk together the vinegar, lemon juice and olive oil and season with salt and pepper. Cut the cooked beetroot into rough chunks, pour over the dressing and toss to coat. Set aside until needed.

Finely slice the Candy Striped and Golden beetroot (a mandoline works best but a sharp knife will do), plunge into a bowl of iced water, leave for 5 minutes then drain and pat dry on kitchen paper.

Spread the cooked beetroot out on a serving platter, sprinkle over the sliced raw beetroot, the apple matchsticks, goat's cheese, basil and pine nuts. Drizzle over any remaining dressing and serve with some crusty bread.

This is one of my friend Jason's recipes. We have it a lot at his and Angela's house and it's one of my favourite salads. I will let him tell it in his own words:

'Now, the star of this show is of course the tomatoes, so try and find yourself a good, ripe selection of as many shapes, sizes and colours as possible. Whatever you do, don't put them anywhere near the fridge. In fact, if it's a nice warm day, pop them in a bowl and put them out to sunbathe for an hour or so. Once the toms are beautifully sun-kissed, chop them up but leave them nice and chunky and give them a good season. I eat this on its own as I'm obsessed with tomatoes, but it works great as a side dish with all kinds of meat and fish.'

Panzanella

SERVES 4 AS A SIDE DISH

2 fist-size pieces of ciabatta bread, or any other unsliced loaf

2 anchovy fillets

3 tablespoons capers

4 tablespoons good olive oil

1 tablespoon red wine vinegar

600 g (1 lb 2 oz) tomatoes, chopped

a bag of mixed salad leaves

salt and pepper

Preheat the oven to 110°C (225°F), gas mark ¼ or its lowest setting.

Rip the bread into bite-size pieces, place on a baking tray and put in the preheated oven for about 20 minutes. Make sure it doesn't burn – what you're looking for is bread that comes out feeling a bit stale.

Meanwhile, put the anchovies, 2 tablespoons of the capers, the oil and vinegar in a pestle and mortar and smash it into a dressing.

Grab yourself a big mixing bowl and put in the tomatoes and bread and pour on the dressing, then get stuck in with your hands. Even give it all a gentle squeeze to make sure the spongy bread soaks up all the juices.

Finally tip your salad leaves on to a serving plate and drop the contents of the bowl over the top, finishing off with the remaining capers.

This is a dish I had to cook on *MasterChef*. I remember thinking it would be easy and smugly set about making it. John looked at his watch and said something about getting the tuna on, and I showed my tuna the pan (I love it rare) and presented it... only to be ripped apart! I had fallen into the restaurant trap, tuna niçoise with a twist, not the classic where you poach the tuna in oil. When I tasted the classic, I saw how wrong mine was, but we are all open to a little interpretation, aren't we?!

Classic salade niçoise

SERVES 4

700 g (1 lb 6 oz) fresh tuna

1 carrot, halved lengthways

1 celery stalk

white of 1 small leek, slit lengthways, but not cut through

a few sprigs of thyme and parsley

1 chilli, deseeded

4 garlic cloves

2 bay leaves

about 750 ml (1¼ pints) olive oil

4 eggs

200 g (7 oz) green beans, blanched

100 g (3½ oz) pitted black olives

6 small vine tomatoes, halved

a handful of fresh basil leaves

16 cooked new potatoes, halved

a handful of flat-leaf parsley

1 small red onion, sliced

about 15 anchovy fillets

salt and pepper

FOR THE DRESSING

3 tablespoons red wine vinegar

1 teaspoon Dijon mustard

1 egg yolk (optional)

250 ml (8 fl oz) olive oil

Trim the tuna and remove all sinews. Put it into a saucepan large enough to fit it easily. Tie the carrot, celery, leek, thyme and parsley tightly in a bundle with some string to make a bouquet garni, and put it in the saucepan along with the chilli, garlic, bay leaves and some seasoning. Cover with olive oil and place the saucepan over a low heat, until it becomes quite volcanic, with big bubbles breaking the surface. At this point take the pan off the heat immediately and let the tuna cool in the liquid.

To make the dressing, blend the vinegar, mustard and egg yolk (if using) in a food processor or blender until the mixture turns white. Then season and, with the machine still running, very slowly add the oil until it is all incorporated.

Boil the eggs for 3–4 minutes, until the yolks are just slightly soft. Cool under cold water and peel off the shells.

When the tuna is cool, remove it from the oil, strain, and, if you like, keep a little of the oil back to stir into the dressing. You can keep the rest in the fridge and use again next time you cook tuna – just make sure you bring it to the boil first, and remove any impurities that come to the surface before you start.

Break the tuna into shards, then mound up with the rest of the ingredients on a big platter or on individual plates and drizzle the dressing over.

When we were little girls, if ever we were off school ill and Mummy was working, Nanna would come to look after us. Victoria and I have such fond memories of these days as we were really made to feel special and were waited on hand and foot. Always on the menu were mugs of hot Ribena and this wonderful potato salad. We would eat bowls and bowls of it... and it always made us feel better!

Warm potato salad

SERVES 4–6

500 g (1 lb) new potatoes, chopped in half if large or left whole if small

2 tablespoons mayonnaise

1 teaspoon Dijon mustard

2 tablespoons freshly chopped chives

1 tablespoon freshly chopped parsley

salt and pepper

Cook the potatoes in a large saucepan of water for about 15–20 minutes until tender.

Drain, and leave to cool slightly, until warm, but not hot.

Tip the potatoes into a large bowl and stir in the mayonnaise, mustard, chives and parsley. Season with salt and pepper and serve straightaway.

VARIATION:
You could also add very thinly sliced preserved lemons (see page 106).

The days are long, the wine is cold, the birds are singing and the bees are buzzing; children are laughing and puppy dogs are wagging their tails on street corners. Life is good when the sun shines and the weather is sweet.

When I was about 21 I spent a lot of time in Paris. I practically lived there on and off for a year. I made two fantastic friends who I used to stay with called Bruno and Jean Pascale (nicknamed KiKi). They lived in Barbès and they used to call me their *petit oiseau* (little bird). We loved all the same music and films; we drank wine, smoked cigarettes and KiKi cooked! He made all sorts of amazing food; I used to sit at his kitchen counter watching him whisk up marinades, cook rabbit and prepare feasts, always saying when dishing it up, 'It's nothing.' They were such happy days – the open windows, the noise of the busy street below, the pure escapism of the millions of French films we watched... I loved that I would leave them, dreaming in French, only to return a week later to their hugs and kisses and culinary delights! This cucumber soup was made in celebration of *le petit oiseau* returning to their nest...

Chilled cucumber soup with salmon roe

SERVES 4

2 large cucumbers, peeled

2 tablespoons rice vinegar

1 garlic clove, peeled

2 large handfuls baby leaf spinach

a small bunch of basil, leaves picked

100 ml (3½ fl oz) Greek-style yogurt

ice cubes

50 g (2 oz) salmon roe

sea salt and white pepper

extra virgin olive oil, to drizzle

Take half of one of the cucumbers, remove the seeds and discard, then cut the flesh into small dice. Place in a bowl with a pinch of salt and pour over the vinegar. Set aside.

Roughly chop the remaining cucumber then tip into a food processor or blender with the garlic, spinach, basil leaves and yogurt. Add a couple of ice cubes and then blitz until smooth. If the soup is too thick, add more ice and keep blending until you reach the desired consistency; it should be slightly thicker than double cream. Season to taste with salt and white pepper and then blitz again.

Drain the diced cucumber, place a spoonful in the centre of 4 chilled serving bowls and then top with a spoonful of the salmon roe.

Pour the soup around the outside then drizzle with a little extra virgin olive oil. Serve immediately.

This recipe really livens up your humble couscous. Great with the lamb tagine (see page 36) or the barbecued sirloin (see page 204) and, needless to say, perfectly suited to a warm, sunny day... yum!

Couscous with pomegranate

SERVES 4–6 AS A SIDE SALAD

400 g (13 oz) couscous

500 ml (17 fl oz) hot vegetable stock

grated zest and juice of 1 lemon

1 teaspoon ras-el-hanout

1 small garlic clove, grated

2 tablespoons extra virgin olive oil

1 large pomegranate, deseeded

½ cucumber, peeled, deseeded and diced

6 radishes, finely sliced

a small bunch of fresh mint, leaves picked and roughly chopped

a small bunch of fresh flat-leaf parsley, leaves picked and roughly chopped

sea salt and pepper

Tip the couscous into a large bowl, pour over the stock and cover with cling film. Leave to stand for 5 minutes. Uncover the bowl, fluff up the grains with a fork and set aside to cool.

Combine the lemon zest and juice, ras-el-hanout, garlic and olive oil in a bowl and whisk to combine. Pour over the couscous and stir to combine. Stir through the remaining ingredients and season to taste.

My friend Jason is a fantastic cook and we love to cook together. He is brilliant at everything but his salads ALWAYS taste amazing. Whenever I ask him about them he says it's because he puts the salad in the microwave! I'm not sure what his secret is but I asked him for his recipe, and here it is in his own words, his brilliant personality stamped all over it, and so I'm not going to mess with it!

Jasee's barmy tuna salad

SERVES 4–6

2 bags of mixed salad leaves

1 x 200 g tin tuna, in spring water if possible, drained

1 x 200 g tin green olives stuffed with anchovies

¼ cucumber

4 tomatoes, quartered

1 red onion (less if you're planning a night of romance), thinly sliced

1 pepper (yellow will make the salad more colourful), deseeded and chopped

40–60 g (1½–2¼ oz) feta cheese

olive oil

balsamic vinegar

salt and pepper

Note: The microwave bit can be avoided by leaving all the ingredients out of the fridge for about an hour before making the salad.

The only bowl that will take a salad this big is a (microwavable) fruit bowl. Tip in the leaves, drained tuna and olives.

Take a peeler and peel the cucumber. Cut in half, scrape out the watery seeds with a teaspoon and discard, then chop the flesh into bite-size pieces. Add the cucumber to the bowl along with the tomatoes, onion and pepper and crumble in the feta.

Dress with a good glug of olive oil, a drizzle of balsamic, season and then mix. Use salad servers if you like, but you'll do a better job if you get stuck in with your hands.

Now for the BARMY bit! Pop the bowl of salad in the microwave for 30–60 seconds. This sounds nuts, but salads taste a million times better when they're not fridge-cold. Room temperature is what you're looking for.

This is another recipe from my lovely friend Dhruv! I don't mean to bang on, but I really am very lucky to be his friend. He lives just down the road from my dad, and I'm always popping in en route, saying 'I'M STARVING!' We actually cooked this dish together at another food festival… but it's his recipe, truly scrumptious and one I have well and truly added to my summer cooking list.

Lamb koftas & baba ganoush

SERVES 4–6

FOR THE KOFTAS

500 g (1 lb) minced lamb

1 teaspoon coriander powder

1 teaspoon cumin powder

1 teaspoon turmeric

1 garlic clove, crushed

juice of 1 lime

1 green chilli, finely chopped

2–3 tablespoons freshly chopped coriander

4–5 teaspoons vegetable oil, for frying

salt and pepper

Flatbreads (see page 11), to serve

FOR THE BABA GANOUSH

2 aubergines

2 garlic cloves

4 tablespoons tahini

juice of 2 lemons

1 teaspoon ground cumin

2 tablespoons olive oil

2 tablespoons freshly chopped parsley

To make the koftas, mix the mince with all the other ingredients, except the oil, in a large bowl and use your hands to form golf ball-size rounds, which you can then mould into kofta shapes. Place the koftas on a baking try and transfer to the fridge to chill for a couple of hours.

Heat the vegetable oil in a deep frying pan until hot. Shallow fry the koftas or cook on a hot barbecue or in an oven preheated to 200°C (400°F), gas mark 6 for 20–25 minutes.

To make the baba ganoush, roast the aubergines directly over a gas flame on the hob (or use a chef's blowtorch if you have one) until the skins are blackened. Leave to cool a bit and then peel the charred skin away.

Put the aubergine flesh into a food processor or blender with the garlic, tahini, lemon juice, cumin and some salt and pepper and blitz to a rough paste. Transfer to a serving dish, drizzle with the olive oil and scatter with the parsley.

Serve the cooked koftas with the baba ganoush and flatbreads.

These are just a couple of marinades for meat and fish that I thought you might like – perfect for perking up a piece of chicken or fish at a moment's notice.

Summer marinades

CHERMOULA

A great marinade for fish or chicken, this sauce can also be spooned over grilled meat, fish or vegetables.

SERVES 4–6 (ENOUGH TO MARINATE 1 KG (2 LB) MEAT)

1 teaspoon cumin seeds

1 teaspoon coriander seeds

2 cloves

a pinch of saffron

1 teaspoon sweet paprika

4 garlic cloves, peeled and left whole

3 red chillies, deseeded and roughly chopped

a large bunch of fresh coriander, leaves and stalks roughly chopped

juice of 1 lemon

100 ml (3½ fl oz) olive oil

sea salt and pepper

Toast the cumin seeds, coriander seeds, cloves and saffron in a dry frying pan over a high heat for a couple of minutes until fragrant. Tip into a spice grinder or pestle and mortar and grind to a fine powder.

Pour the spice mix and all of the remaining ingredients into a food processor or blender and blitz until smooth. Season to taste with plenty of salt and pepper.

JERK MARINADE

Traditionally used for chicken, this also works with pork, fish and vegetables. This recipe uses quite a lot of fiery Scotch bonnet chillies but you can use milder chillies if you prefer.

SERVES 4–6 (ENOUGH TO MARINATE 1 KG (2 LB) MEAT)

6 Scotch bonnet chillies, deseeded and chopped

a large bunch of spring onions, roughly chopped

6 garlic cloves, peeled and left whole

5 cm (2 inch) piece of fresh ginger, peeled and roughly chopped

2 teaspoons dark muscovado sugar

grated rind and juice of 1 orange

grated rind and juice of 1 lime

3 thyme sprigs, leaves picked

2 teaspoons ground allspice

1 teaspoon ground cinnamon

1 teaspoon ground nutmeg

1 teaspoon freshly ground black pepper

1 teaspoon sea salt flakes

100 ml (3½ fl oz) white wine vinegar

100 ml (3½ fl oz) olive oil

Pour all the ingredients into a food processor or blender and blitz until smooth. Slash chicken pieces (or other meat of your choice) all over with a sharp knife, pour over the marinade, cover and refrigerate for 3–4 hours, or overnight if possible, before cooking.

This is a really lovely recipe from my best friend Emma's husband, Dan. His mother is a fab cook and so is my friend Em, but Dan loves his food and he is always in charge of the barbecue on a sunny day. He loves food, rugby, beer, his family and his home; he is what I call a 'proper man', a provider, a looker-afterer, and I adore him and his lamb!

Dan's lamb

SERVES 8–10

I whole leg of lamb, butterflied

2 lemons

I tablespoon salt

fresh thyme leaves

250 ml (8 fl oz) natural yogurt

2 red chillies, deseeded

fresh coriander, chopped

2 garlic cloves

a pinch of salt and pepper

I tablespoon cinnamon

½ tablespoon each of cardamom, cloves and turmeric

fresh rosemary sprigs

8–10 Flatbreads (see page II), to serve

FOR THE TZATZIKI

2 garlic cloves

300 g (10 oz) natural yogurt

juice of I lemon

a small handful of fresh mint leaves, chopped

First tenderise the lamb by rubbing it with the juice from I of the lemons, some salt and some thyme leaves. Leave for a few hours.

To make the tzatziki, crush the garlic with a little salt in a pestle and mortar until it forms a paste. Add to the yogurt and lemon juice and stir well. Stir through the mint. Set aside until needed.

Put the remaining ingredients, except the rosemary, in a food processor or blender and blitz to make a paste. Rub the marinade into the lamb and cover with some sprigs of rosemary. Cover with cling film and leave in the fridge overnight.

Barbecue the lamb on a hot grill for 30 minutes and then move to one side and leave to cook for another 30 minutes if you like your meat pink. Finish with the juice from the remaining lemon and leave to rest for about 10 minutes before slicing it.

Serve the lamb with flatbreads and the tzatziki.

Obviously this recipe is in the 'sunshine chapter', where the days are long, the wine is cold, the birds are singing and the bees are buzzing; children are laughing and puppy dogs are wagging their tails on street corners. Life is good when the sun shines and the weather is sweet, as the song goes. But back to reality – and it's pouring with rain! So feel free to use the grill or oven for this one if the sun's not shining where you are…

Barbecued sirloin with harissa paste

SERVES 4–6

2 kg (4 lb) boneless beef sirloin
sea salt and pepper

FOR THE HARISSA PASTE

1 whole garlic bulb

1 red pepper, left whole

1 tablespoon cumin seeds

1 tablespoon caraway seeds

1 teaspoon rock salt

1 tablespoon sherry vinegar

2 teaspoons smoked paprika

3 tablespoons extra virgin olive oil

½ teaspoon caster sugar

1 tablespoon tomato purée

10 red chillies, deseeded and roughly chopped

2 tablespoons small dried rose petals (optional)

Preheat the oven to 200°C (400°F), gas mark 6.

Wrap the garlic in foil and place on a baking tray with the red pepper. Roast in the oven for 30 minutes.

Put the roasted pepper in a large bowl, cover with cling film and leave for 10 minutes. Remove the cling film and, when cool enough to handle, peel the charred skin and deseed.

Unwrap the garlic from the foil and squeeze the soft flesh into the bowl of a food processor or blender. Add the roasted pepper flesh and the remaining harissa paste ingredients and blitz until smooth. Season to taste with some salt and pepper and then set aside one-quarter of the paste to be used as a dipping sauce.

Lay the beef on a large roasting tray and rub the remaining harissa paste all over, ensuring it is well covered. Cover with cling film and leave to marinate in the fridge for 6 hours, or overnight if possible.

Prepare your barbecue when you are ready to cook. Remove the beef from the fridge at least 1 hour before cooking.

Sear the beef on a hot barbecue grill for 3 minutes on each side and then cover with the lid and roast for 40 minutes, turning often, or until cooked to your liking. Transfer to a roasting tray, cover with foil and leave to rest for 15 minutes.

Carve the beef into thick slices and serve with the remaining harissa paste and a crisp green salad.

Last summer I did a show with Matt Dawson. We hit it off immediately and spent quite a lot of time in our caravan talking food. It was lovely to meet someone who had gone through the same food 'journey' as me and was equally passionate about it. Apart from one day of pure rain, my memories of filming are of glorious sunshine (though I think it may be my mind playing tricks!). I remember chatting about what we were going to do when we got home and Matt said he was going to make beer-can chicken... my ears pricked up! I had never heard of this before, and when he explained the process to me I couldn't wait to get home and try it. You are meant to cook it on a barbie, but of course by the time I returned home the rain had set in. The oven worked just as well! So here is Matt's take on this very clever recipe, which has now become one of my staple summer dishes.

Beer-can chicken

SERVES 4–6

1 x 1.5 kg (3 lb) chicken

1 tablespoon freshly chopped rosemary

grated zest and juice of 1 lemon (reserve one half)

3 garlic bulbs, cloves smashed but skin on

2 tablespoons olive oil

1 can of lager

salt and pepper

Put the chicken in a large plastic bag and add some salt and pepper, the chopped rosemary, lemon zest and juice, garlic and olive oil and leave to marinate for a good 2 hours.

When you are ready to cook prepare the barbecue to a high heat, or preheat the oven to 200°C (400°F), gas mark 6.

Crack open a can of lager and drink one-third of it. Put the can on a baking tray and place half a lemon on the can. Stuff the chicken with all the bits and bobs from the marinade and then perch the bird on the can so that it sits upright with the can in its cavity. Use the chicken's legs as a tripod to stand securely with the can. Drop the lid of the barbecue or close the oven door and leave the chicken to steam roast for about 1–1½ hours. Try not to lift the lid or open the door too much. Baste occasionally with the tray juices.

Serve with rice or potato salad.

When I was growing up, pork pies were a staple on family picnics and trips to my grandparents' beach hut. Even at the age of seven I loved them with a tiny scraping of mustard! My favourite bit of course was the jelly and the pastry. I used to pull out the meat and eat that first with the mustard and then really take my time over the jelly and crispy pastry. I have used a quick jelly here, and the pie is a big fella, so feel free to halve the quantities and make a smaller version… I suppose as I wrote this, I had big summer parties in mind!

Pork pie

SERVES 12

FOR THE FILLING

100 g (3½ oz) streaky bacon, chopped

1 small ham hock, meat removed

300 g (10 oz) boned pork shoulder, diced to 1 cm (½ inch) pieces

¼ teaspoon mace

a pinch of ground nutmeg

¼ teaspoon ground allspice

½ tablespoon freshly chopped sage

½ tablespoon freshly chopped parsley

1 fresh thyme stalk, leaves only

a pinch each of fine salt and ground white pepper

1 teaspoon mustard powder

FOR THE QUICK JELLY

150 ml (¼ pint) hot ham stock (use a ham stock cube) or chicken stock

150 ml (¼ pint) apple juice

3 gelatine leaves

a handful of parsley, chopped

First make the jelly. Heat the ham stock with the apple juice in a small saucepan. Soak the gelatine leaves in a little bowl of cold water for a couple of minutes, then remove and squeeze out as much water as possible. Add to the hot stock and apple and allow to melt. Remove from the heat, stir in the parsley and set aside.

For the filling, blitz the bacon and ham hock meat with one-third of the pork shoulder in a food processor or blender, then add to the rest of the meat in a large bowl along with the seasonings and herbs and leave to rest for an hour or so.

Preheat the oven to 200°C (400°F), gas mark 6. Fold pieces of foil into strips (you will need to make 24). Take a 12-hole muffin tin or 12 metal pudding moulds and line each with 2 strips of tin foil, at crisscrosses to each other so they stick up above the level of the tins. This will give you something to hold on to, to remove your pies from the moulds.

To make the hot-water crust pastry, sift the flour, salt and icing sugar into a bowl and make a well in the centre. Put the lard, butter and water in a saucepan and heat until the lard and butter have melted, then increase the heat and bring to a rolling boil. Pour into the bowl with the flour and mix quickly until it forms a paste, then knead until smooth. You need to use it before it cools.

CONTINUED OVERLEAF

Pork pie continued

FOR THE PASTRY

500 g (1 lb) plain flour

1½ teaspoons salt

1 tablespoon icing sugar

100 g (3½ oz) lard, chopped

100 g (3½ oz) cold butter, cubed

100 ml (3½ fl oz) water

1 egg, beaten

Take two-thirds of the pastry and divide into 12 equal portions. Roll each one out and line your prepared tin or moulds. Bring the pastry up the sides to just above the level of the rim. Make sure there are no cracks or gaps.

Divide the remaining pastry into 12 and roll out to make lids just a little larger than the top of your pies.

Fill the tins with the meat filling, doming it up slightly in the centre to act as a support for the lid. Brush the edges with beaten egg, put the lid on top and use your fingers to crimp and seal the lid in place.

Trim any excess pastry and brush all over with beaten egg. Make a small hole in the centre of each one to allow the steam to escape. Bake for 15 minutes, then reduce the temperature to 160°C (325°F), gas mark 3 and bake for a further 30 minutes, or until the filling is piping hot in the centre when tested with a skewer. You don't want to overcook the pies or they will become dry.

Stand for 15–20 minutes and then very carefully remove the pies from the tins using the foil strips to help you. Brush all over with beaten egg and return to the oven for 10 minutes to glaze the outside of the pies.

Leave them to cool for a good hour, until just warm, then use a funnel to pour the jelly into each pie (if the jelly has set, just warm it to liquid in a saucepan). Chill for at least 3 hours to set the jelly before serving.

I have memories of lying on a very quiet beach in Lanzarote. Billie was very young and sleeping in her buggy with a towel shading her. I was on a towel on the sand, reading a book, when I suddenly caught the smell of barbecued fish on the air… I sat up to see where it was coming from, and just by the little beach café, a fisherman (who I later found out to be the café owner) was grilling sardines on the back of a disused fishing boat. A while later we walked over; all the sardines bar one were gone but he said he had something else and invited us to sit down. He had some fresh squid and the sardine and a few other bits of fish, which he gave to his wife, and within a few minutes there was a basket of fresh fried fish in a light batter served with the biggest, brightest lemons I'd ever seen. With twinkling eyes and a thick Spanish accent he declared, 'Frito mixto!'

Frito mixto

SERVES 4–6

2 litres (3½ pints) vegetable oil

6 large raw prawns, shells removed and cleaned

flour, for dusting

2 squid, cut into rings 2.5 cm (1 inch) thick

200 g (7 oz) white fish, cut into strips

6 small scallops, halved

3 lemons

FOR THE BATTER

50 g (2 oz) self-raising flour

150 g (5 oz) cornflour

1 teaspoon salt

300 ml (½ pint) cold soda water

1 egg white, whisked

Make the batter about an hour before you want to eat – it will settle, but then can be stirred up when you are ready to fry. Gradually beat the flour, cornflour and salt into the soda water in a bowl. Add the whisked egg white and keep beating until a creamy batter is formed.

Preheat the oven to 160°C (325°F), gas mark 3.

Heat the oil in a deep frying pan or saucepan and have a plate ready with kitchen paper on, to drain the fried fish. Get all the food ready as you will fry the seafood in batches.

Coat the prawns lightly in flour and then in the batter. Gently place them in the hot oil and fry for 4 minutes until they start to float.

Remove the prawns from the pan and let the oil come back up to temperature before frying the squid, for about 3 minutes, and then the fish and scallops for 3 minutes each. Keep all the food warm in the oven if necessary. Serve with lemon wedges.

I first made this while camping in Cornwall, spreading great big sea bass over three mini throwaway barbecues. It's very simple and delicious; the preserved lemons add a more delicate flavour to the dish but feel free to use fresh lemons. You can also substitute the herbs too – coriander and mint work well with this dish. Play around with this recipe, as it's all down to your own personal taste.

Whole sea bass with salsa verde

SERVES 4

25 g (1 oz) Preserved Lemons (see page 106), sliced

1 garlic clove, sliced

a small bunch each of fresh parsley, tarragon, mint and basil

2 sea bass, weighing about 400–600 g (13–18 oz) each, heads on but gutted

olive oil, for rubbing

FOR THE SALSA VERDE

2 teaspoons freshly chopped tarragon

2 teaspoons freshly chopped chervil

2 teaspoons freshly chopped chives

1 garlic clove, chopped

grated zest and juice of 1 lemon, plus more grated zest to serve

25 g (1 oz) capers, roughly chopped

100 ml (3½ fl oz) olive oil

salt and pepper

Put half the preserved lemons, the garlic slices and a sprinkling of each of the herbs inside each of the sea bass.

To make the salsa verde, mix the herbs, garlic, lemon zest and juice, capers and olive oil together and season to taste.

Score slashes into the skin and flesh of both sides of the fish. Rub with a little olive oil and then rub all over with the salsa verde, getting as much into the cuts as possible.

Preheat the grill to medium (or use a barbecue in the summer) and cook for about 8 minutes on each side. Alternatively, preheat the oven to 180°C (350°F), gas mark 4 and cook the fish on a baking tray for about 12 minutes. The fish will be ready when the thickest part of the flesh is opaque. Serve with buttered new potatoes and a sprinkling of lemon zest.

It's funny how your tastes change as you get older. Up until a few years ago the idea of a lemon dessert was not a nice one to me. However, last year on a trip to Avignon with my sister I tasted the lightest, most delicate lemon tart in the whole of France and it completely blew all my preconceived 'lemon' ideas out of the water! I've tried to recreate it here to see if it can invoke some sunshine...

Tarte au citron

SERVES 8

FOR THE SWEET PASTRY

175 g (6 oz) plain flour

20 g (¾ oz) icing sugar

100 g (3½ oz) butter

1 egg yolk

1 tablespoon water

FOR THE FILLING

juice of 4 good-sized lemons

100 g (3½ oz) caster sugar

125 ml (4 fl oz) crème fraîche

5 eggs

Put the flour, icing sugar and butter into a food processor and pulse until the mixture resembles coarse breadcrumbs.

Add the egg yolk and water and pulse again, just until the mixture holds together. Tip the mix on to greaseproof paper and flatten to a disc. Cover with another sheet of greaseproof paper and carefully transfer to the fridge to chill for 30 minutes. Meanwhile, preheat the oven to 200°C (400°F), gas mark 6.

Remove the dough from the fridge and, leaving it between the 2 pieces of greaseproof paper, roll out the disc to a slightly larger circle than a 23 cm (9 inch) tart tin. Use the pastry to line the tin and then bake blind in the preheated oven for 12–15 minutes.

Remove the baking beans from the pastry and return the tart to the oven for a further 5–10 minutes. Leave to cool before filling. Reduce the oven temperature to 190°C (375°F), gas mark 5.

While the pastry is cooling, make the filling. Using a wire whisk, whisk the lemon juice, sugar and crème fraîche together in a bowl. Whisk in the eggs one at a time.

Pour the lemon cream into the cooled tart shell and bake for 15–20 minutes until firm.

I first made mint panna cotta at a pop-up restaurant in Soho. Really light and refreshing, it is beautifully complemented by the strawberries – macerating strawberries is a great way to sweeten and 'juice up' the fruit. A proper summer dessert!

Mint panna cotta with strawberries

SERVES 4

FOR THE PANNA COTTA

4 gelatine leaves

250 ml (8 fl oz) double cream

250 ml (8 fl oz) milk

1 vanilla pod, split lengthways

2 fresh mint sprigs, plus extra to decorate (optional)

50 g (2 oz) caster sugar

FOR THE STRAWBERRIES

400 g (13 oz) strawberries, halved or quartered

1 tablespoon balsamic vinegar

juice of 1 lemon

2 tablespoons caster sugar

To make the panna cotta, first soak the gelatine in a bowl of cold water until soft.

Place the cream, milk, vanilla pod and seeds, mint sprigs and sugar into a saucepan and bring to a simmer. Turn off the heat and leave in the saucepan with some cling film covering the pan tightly. Leave the mint to infuse for about 5 minutes, but make sure the milk is still warm. Pick out the vanilla pod and the mint.

Squeeze out the soaked gelatine and add to the saucepan. Stir to dissolve.

Divide the mixture between 4 ramekin or glass dishes. Leave to cool and set in the fridge for 2 hours, or overnight.

To prepare the strawberries, mix together the vinegar, lemon juice and sugar. Put the strawberries in a bowl and pour over the liquid; stir to combine. Leave in the fridge for 2–3 hours.

Serve the strawberries on top or around the panna cotta when set and decorate with mint leaves, if liked.

I wanted to include these in this chapter as they conjure up memories of Spanish holidays as a child. Every year we would be whisked off with literally a day's notice after my mum had found a deal at the travel agent's. It was always Spain, and Victoria and I loved it. Days on the beach, in and out of the sea, followed by dinners in a nearby town… an orange or lemon sorbet was nearly always our dessert of choice; we would select them from the photos on the menu and loved that they came inside the 'shell' of the fruit, as these do here!

Orange, lemon & lime sorbets

SERVES 4–6

200 g (7 oz) caster sugar

150 ml (¼ pint) water

600 ml (1 pint) freshly squeezed orange juice, strained to get rid of pith and pips (about 3 oranges), reserving the shells

juice of ½ a lemon, or to taste

ORANGE SORBET

Place the sugar and water in a small saucepan and simmer for 5–10 minutes until syrupy. Remove from the heat and cool. Stir the orange juice into the syrup. Pour into an ice-cream machine and churn according to the manufacturer's instructions, then scoop into the shells of the orange and freeze until ready to serve.

SERVES 4–6

250 g (8 oz) caster sugar

500 ml (17 fl oz) water

250 ml (8 fl oz) freshly squeezed lemon juice, strained to get rid of pith and pips (about 5–6 lemons), reserving the shells

LEMON SORBET

Place the sugar and half the water in a small saucepan and simmer for 5–10 minutes until syrupy. Remove from the heat and cool. Mix the remaining water with the lemon juice into the cooled syrup. Pour into an ice-cream machine and churn according to the manufacturer's instructions. Scoop into the empty lemon shells and freeze until ready to serve.

SERVES 4–6

250 g (8 oz) caster sugar

500 ml (17 fl oz) water

200 ml (7 fl oz) freshly squeezed lime juice, strained to get rid of pith and pips (about 5 limes), reserving the shells

juice of 1 lemon

LIME SORBET

Place the sugar and half the water in a small saucepan and simmer for 5–10 minutes until syrupy. Remove from the heat and cool. Stir the remaining water with the lime juice into the syrup. Pour into an ice-cream machine and churn according to the manufacturer's instructions. Scoop into the shells of the limes and freeze until ready to serve.

These are such a lovely summertime dessert – serve in wine glasses or in little jam jars or Kilner jars and take them on picnics.

Champagne & elderflower jellies

SERVES 4

6 gelatine leaves

100 ml (3½ fl oz) water

600 ml (1 pint) champagne, prosecco or sparkling wine

60 g (2¼ oz) caster sugar

2 tablespoons elderflower cordial, or to taste

Soak the gelatine leaves in a bowl of cold water for about 5 minutes.

Put the water, 150 ml (¼ pint) of the champagne or sparkling wine and the sugar in a saucepan over a medium heat and heat until hot and the sugar has dissolved. Remove from the heat.

Squeeze the excess water from the gelatine leaves and add to the saucepan, stirring until these have also dissolved.

Pour the liquid into a measuring jug, add the elderflower cordial and top up to 800 ml (1⅓ pints) with the remaining champagne. Leave to cool and then pour into serving glasses or jars. Transfer to the fridge to set for about 4 hours.

THE WAY I COOK...

with a House Full of Kids

I love a full house! Friends, family and children, I'm not fussy. My own or other people's, I just like that noise, that constant chatter and banging and whirlwind of dressing up, Lego, Barbie dolls and musical instruments, minor earthquakes to deal with, muddy shoes, bloody knees and cries of 'I'm hungry!'... This chapter isn't only about the way I cook for children; it includes recipes for things to cook with them, too. The main points to remember: all mess can be cleaned up and food doesn't have to be perfect. Oh, and the more kids actually cook, the more they are likely to eat. Enjoy!

I recently went to Berlin for my best friend Nicola's hen do. We stayed in the most beautiful hotel, where we had our own cocktail waiter who mixed us drinks while we got ready for our night out. There was a fabulous claw-footed bath in our room and Nicola sat immersed in bubbles drinking Soho Mules! Aside from the decadence, we went exploring and ended up in a place called Friedrichshain. We were starving and a little hungover and started looking for somewhere to eat – a guy came out of one of the bars with a great big grin and asked us if we wanted a table. There was one left in the shade, which he promptly moved into the spring sunshine. We asked him what their speciality was and he told us about the *flammkuchen*. He brought us out three cold beers and a huge plate of what looked like a pizza bianco, although it was much thinner and crispier and creamy and oniony and delicious. We fell in love with it and as soon as I arrived home I made it. The kids love it too!

Flammkuchen

SERVES 4

250 g (8 oz) strong white bread flour, plus extra for dusting

½ x 7 g sachet dried yeast

1 teaspoon caster sugar

1 tablespoon olive oil

6 tablespoons cold water

1 teaspoon salt

FOR THE TOPPING

150 ml (¼ pint) crème fraîche

2 shallots, finely sliced into rings

4 rashers smoked bacon, speck or pancetta

1 tablespoon freshly chopped chives

salt and pepper

Preheat the oven to 220°C (425°F), gas mark 7.

Put 50 g (2 oz) of the flour, the yeast, sugar, olive oil and 4 tablespoons of the water in a bowl and mix together. Cover with cling film and leave to prove for about 30 minutes.

Add the rest of the flour, about 2 tablespoons more water and the salt to the proved mixture and mix to a dough. Turn out on to a lightly floured surface and knead for about 10 minutes – or if you have a stand mixer with a dough hook mix for about 10 minutes. The dough should be quite sticky and elastic.

Divide the dough in half and then roll out on to 2 floured baking sheets. The dough should be as thin as possible.

Spread over the crème fraîche, sprinkle with the shallots and bacon and a good grind of salt and pepper. Bake in the preheated oven for about 7 minutes. Sprinkle with the chopped chives and serve.

I could eat these croquettes all day and all night for the whole year, they are that delicious and I love them *that* much! They make a great starter or tapas-type lunch; I have included them in this chapter as they are a favourite of my nieces, too.

Ham & cheese croquettes

SERVES 4–6 AS A STARTER
OR SNACK

50 g (2 oz) unsalted butter

50 g (2 oz) plain flour, plus
extra for dusting

450 ml (¾ pint) warm milk

100 g (3½ oz) Manchego cheese,
grated

75 g (3 oz) Serrano ham or
other cured ham, finely chopped

vegetable oil, for deep-frying

I egg, beaten

75 g (3 oz) panko breadcrumbs
or other dried white
breadcrumbs

a pinch of sea salt flakes

a pinch of smoked paprika
(possibly leave this out for
children)

Note: For kids in big shoes, serve
with a glass of sherry.

Melt the butter in a saucepan over a medium heat, add the flour and cook for 5 minutes, stirring constantly, until the mixture starts to turn golden brown.

Gradually whisk in the warm milk and then cook the mixture gently, stirring regularly, for 10 minutes; the sauce should be thick and glossy. Remove the pan from the heat and beat in the cheese and ham.

Lightly oil a small baking tin, pour the mixture in, then press a sheet of cling film on to the surface (this will prevent a skin from forming). Transfer to the fridge and chill for 2 hours, or overnight, until set.

Heat the oil for deep-frying to 180°C (350°F). Flour your hands and then take a heaped teaspoonful of the mixture and roll it into a ball. Flatten the sides slightly to form a barrel shape. Put some flour, the beaten egg and breadcrumbs in 3 separate shallow dishes. Dip each croquette in the flour, followed by the egg and then the breadcrumbs, tapping off any excess as you go. Repeat with the remaining mixture.

Drop a small cube of bread in to the hot oil to check the temperature – it should start to sizzle and brown if the oil is hot enough. When the oil is ready, deep-fry the croquettes in batches for 2 minutes until golden brown and crisp. Drain on kitchen paper.

While the croquettes are still hot, sprinkle with a little salt and smoked paprika, if using. Serve warm.

I first made these when Billie was a toddler. I had forgotten about them until about a year ago when I was thinking of something different to make for her dinner and I remembered how much she loved them. They are delicious, easy to whizz up in a food processor and make a nice alternative to beef.

Chicken burgers & sweet potato wedges

SERVES 6

FOR THE BURGERS

4 chicken breast fillets

½ onion

1 garlic clove, grated

1 tablespoon freshly chopped coriander

grated zest of 1 lemon

1 egg

25–40 g (1–1½ oz) breadcrumbs

oil, for frying

salt and pepper

FOR THE WEDGES

6 sweet potatoes

olive oil, for drizzling

Chop the chicken in a food processor until it is minced, then set aside in a large bowl.

Put the onion in the food processor and chop until really fine and almost liquid. Add the onion to the bowl of chicken along with the garlic, chopped coriander, lemon zest, egg, breadcrumbs and some salt and pepper and mix to combine.

Shape the mixture into 6 burgers, put on a floured plate and refrigerate for 30 minutes to firm.

Meanwhile, cook the wedges. Preheat the oven to 190–200°C (375–400°F), gas mark 5–6. Cut the sweet potatoes into wedges, leaving the skin on. Arrange on a baking tray and drizzle with olive oil. Bake in the preheated oven for about 30–40 minutes, until soft.

When the burgers have firmed, heat a good glug of oil in a frying pan over a medium heat and add the burgers. Cook for about 6 minutes on each side.

Serve in buns with salad and the sweet potato wedges – or Billie likes them with noodles and spicy coleslaw too!

In my last book I included my mum's recipe for Rice Krispie Chicken. It has always caused a little bit of a stir – people can be very reticent 'Rice Krispies..? And mayonnaise...?? On chicken???' – until they try it! Well, it seems my mum wasn't the only one using cereal in the 80s. This is a recipe from my friend, and brilliant home economist, Rich's mum. She used cornflakes! This has now become a firm favourite in our household.

Crispy cornflake chicken

SERVES 4—6

olive oil

250 g (8 oz) cornflakes

I egg

50 g (2 oz) plain flour, plus extra for dusting

125 ml (4 fl oz) milk

I teaspoon cayenne pepper, or to taste

8 skinless chicken pieces (thighs, drumsticks or a mixture)

sea salt and pepper

salad and garlic mayonnaise, to serve

Preheat the oven to 180°C (350°F), gas mark 4 and lightly grease 2 baking sheets with olive oil.

Pour the cornflakes into a large sandwich bag; seal and then lightly crush with a rolling pin. Pour into a large flat dish or roasting tin and set aside.

In a large bowl, whisk together the egg, flour, milk and cayenne pepper until smooth. Put the chicken pieces into a bag with a dusting of flour and plenty of salt and pepper. Seal the bag and shake to coat the chicken evenly.

Dip each chicken piece in the egg and milk mixture first and then roll it in the crushed cornflakes, making sure each piece is evenly coated.

Lay the coated chicken on the prepared baking trays and then transfer to the preheated oven for 40 minutes or until the chicken is cooked through.

Serve with a side salad and some garlic mayonnaise.

Believe me there is nothing wrong with the humble shop-bought fish finger straight from the freezer. I love them, especially in a sandwich with lots of ketchup and mayo and a slice of cheese! But sometimes it's really nice to make your own, not least because it's something you can actually get the kids involved in, and, as I've said before, anything that gets children cooking and interested in food is a big plus in my book. These fish fingers can be as regimented as you want – if you use almost frozen fish you can cut proper shaped fish fingers, or you can simply make different shapes and call them goujons! Whatever way you choose, they are delicious… and because you made them yourself, you know exactly what's in them.

Homemade fish fingers

SERVES 4

500 g (1 lb) cod or haddock fillet

grated zest of 1 lemon

about 200 g (7 oz) fresh or dried breadcrumbs

about 50 g (2 oz) plain flour

2 eggs, beaten

salt and pepper

Preheat the oven to 220°C (425°F), gas mark 7.

Cut the fish into strips the length of the fillet and cut across evenly so that you have fish finger-sized portions.

Mix the lemon zest, breadcrumbs and some salt and pepper together in a large bowl. Put the flour and the beaten eggs in 2 separate shallow dishes. Dip the fish first into the flour, then the egg, then the breadcrumbs, tapping off the excess as you go. Place the fish fingers on a greased baking sheet and then chill in the fridge for at least 20 minutes.

Cook in the preheated oven for about 12–15 minutes until golden and crispy.

Serve the fish fingers with baked beans and chips, or – my favourite – in a sandwich of sliced white bread, spread with mayo and ketchup and a slice of cheese.

I have battled with myself as to whether this actually counts as a recipe! When we were late getting home and needed a very quick tea, my mum would make this. Obviously, loaded potato skins are very easy and you can fill them with whatever you like, but my reason for including them was a conversation with a cab driver about how his son wouldn't eat a single vegetable, including potato, unless it was a chip. I'd suggested that this would be a good thing to try, seeing as he could make and prepare it himself and that he liked cheese – I wonder how he got on!

Loaded potato skins with bacon, cheese & spring onions

SERVES 4

oil, for frying

100 g (3½ oz) pancetta, cubed

4 spring onions, chopped

4 jacket potatoes, baked (either half in the microwave and half in the oven or solely in the oven because you need a crispy skin)

4 knobs of butter

100 g (3½ oz) Cheddar cheese, grated

salt and pepper

Heat some oil in a frying pan over a medium heat and fry the pancetta cubes and spring onions for a few minutes.

Cut the cooked baked potatoes in half and scoop the insides into a bowl. Add the butter, pancetta and spring onions, cheese (keeping a handful back) and some salt and pepper. Mix together and spoon back into the halved potato skins.

Preheat the grill to medium.

Sprinkle the top of each potato skin with the remaining cheese and place under the preheated grill. Cook until the cheese starts to bubble and the top goes a little crispy.

I couldn't leave this one out! The only decision was whether to put it into 'For Family and Friends' or this chapter. Everybody has their own way of making this classic, and that's what I love about this dish (and home cooking in general) – there is no hard and fast rule. Have a read of this recipe and take from it what you want. My secret is to cook the onions really slowly, to take your time and lovingly make this dish. One last thing: I often double up on the ingredients and freeze a batch.

Spag bol

SERVES 4

2 tablespoons oil

1 onion, finely chopped

1 garlic clove, crushed

1 teaspoon dried oregano

1 teaspoon dried thyme

1 teaspoon dried marjoram

500 g (1 lb) lean minced beef

75 g (3 oz) pancetta cubes (optional)

2 tablespoons tomato purée

1 teaspoon Marmite

1 large glass red wine

1 x 400 g tin chopped tomatoes

1 dessertspoon sugar

salt and pepper

cooked spaghetti, to serve

Pour the oil into a large heavy-based saucepan and warm over a low-medium heat. Add the onion and cook slowly until it really starts to soften – the slower you cook your onion, the sweeter and more flavoursome it will become.

Add the garlic and herbs and then turn up the heat and add the mince. Really bash down the meat to brown it evenly. Add the pancetta, if using.

Stir in the tomato purée, Marmite and wine and let that bubble away for a few minutes. Add the tomatoes, turn the heat down to low and let the sauce bubble away for a good 30 minutes.

Taste the sauce at this point – this is when I usually add the sugar and salt and pepper and see if it needs anything else. The sauce is pretty much done, though I think the longer and slower you let it cook, the better it tastes – it also tastes even better the next day! Serve with spaghetti.

I first learnt how to make this pasta when I went on a cookery show with Ed Baines. This is one the kids can really get involved in: especially when you push the pasta down and make the pig's ear shapes with your thumbs. It has become a real favourite in our house and the simple pasta sauce can be used as a base for anything.

Orecchiette with tomato & basil sauce

SERVES 6–8

FOR THE SAUCE

800 g (1 lb 10 oz) very ripe tomatoes, the best you can find

3 garlic cloves, unpeeled

a bunch of fresh basil, leaves torn and stalks finely chopped

1 tablespoon caster sugar

1 tablespoon sherry vinegar

2 tablespoons olive oil

sea salt and pepper

FOR THE ORECCHIETTE

500 g (1 lb) fine semolina flour, plus extra for dusting

a pinch of fine sea salt

225 ml (7½ fl oz) warm water

finely grated Parmesan cheese, to serve

Note: This is a great way to use up lots of leftover, overripe tomatoes. I tend to make a large batch of the sauce and freeze half – always handy if you need a tasty meal in a hurry!

First, make the sauce. Preheat the oven to 160°C (325°F), gas mark 3. Tip all the sauce ingredients into a large roasting tray. Season and toss everything together. Roast for 1 hour, shaking the tray occasionally, until the tomatoes are soft.

Leave to cool, then slip the garlic out of their skins. Tip the tomatoes, garlic and roasting juices into a food processor or blender and blitz. Taste and check the seasoning, adding a little extra sugar and vinegar if necessary. Set aside until needed (this can be made ahead and stored in the fridge).

To make the orecchiette, pour the flour and salt into a bowl, make a well in the middle and gradually pour in the warm water, mixing with a fork. Once all of the water is combined, tip the mixture on to a floured work surface and knead for 2–3 minutes until the dough is smooth and elastic. Wrap the dough in cling film and refrigerate for 1–2 hours until firm.

Roll the dough out on a floured surface until around 1½ cm (¾ inch) thick and then cut into 1½ cm (¾ inch) wide strips. Roll each strip lightly into a long sausage shape then cut into small lengths, again around 1½ cm (¾ inch). Using your thumb, press down on each piece of dough to form a small 'ear' shape. Repeat with the remaining dough, dusting the pieces with flour to stop them from sticking to each other.

Pour the sauce into a large wide pan and bring to a simmer. Bring a large pan of salted water to the boil, add the pasta and cook for 2 minutes or until al dente. Add a ladleful of the cooking water to the sauce then drain the pasta and add to the pan. Stir to combine and then serve immediately with a sprinkling of grated Parmesan and a crisp green salad.

While I was filming in America for *This Morning* putting together a strand called 'Movie Star Menus', we travelled to LA, San Francisco, Connecticut and New York. It was a really lovely trip! It really refuelled my love for all things American and a lot of this book has a nod to American cuisine. However, when I was in the little town of Mystic (home of the film and the restaurant Mystic Pizza) I was taught this lovely meatball dish. Wedding meatballs are usually served in a soup, but I decided to serve them with classic marinara sauce and spaghetti.

Wedding meatballs & marinara sauce

SERVES 4

400 g (13 oz) minced beef

90 g (3½ oz) minced chicken

90 g (3½ oz) minced sausagemeat

3 tablespoons grated Parmesan cheese

1 egg

4 tablespoons fresh or dried breadcrumbs

1 garlic clove, crushed

3 pinches of dried oregano

1 tablespoon double cream

1 teaspoon salt

1 teaspoon freshly ground black pepper

1 quantity Mystic Pizza Tomato Sauce (see page 13), to serve

cooked spaghetti, to serve

Preheat the oven to 180°C (350°F), gas mark 4.

Put the minced beef, chicken and sausagemeat in a bowl and add the cheese, egg, breadcrumbs, garlic, oregano, double cream, salt and pepper. Use your hands to mix it all together.

Tear off a small amount and roll it into a ball. Do the same with the rest of the mixture and put the meatballs in a roasting tray. Bake in the preheated oven for about 9 minutes until the meatballs are cooked through.

Try these meatballs with my Mystic Pizza Tomato Sauce.

VARIATION: To make a meatball grinder, put the meatballs in a bread roll of your choice and top with sauce.

My very first modelling job was for *Just 17* magazine – at the time this was my favourite mag and to be asked to do the cover was a really big thing for me! After the first cover shoot they decided to take me away on a photo assignment to Mexico. I was just 17 myself at the time and so excited! We had a ball out there... apart from being held up at knifepoint in Mexico City... and I fell in love with the country, and the food. I remember having these in a market and dipping them in really bitter hot chocolate, feeling terribly grown-up and worldly-wise. The joys of youth!

Churros & proper hot chocolate

SERVES 4

FOR THE CHURROS

125 ml (4 fl oz) whole milk

125 ml (4 fl oz) water

100 g (3½ oz) unsalted butter

1 teaspoon caster sugar, plus extra for dusting

a pinch of salt

150 g (5 oz) plain flour, sifted

4 eggs

vegetable oil, for deep-frying

FOR THE HOT CHOCOLATE

150 g (5 oz) dark chocolate, broken into pieces

2 teaspoons caster sugar

400 ml (14 fl oz) whole milk

200 ml (7 fl oz) double cream

Note: For kids in big shoes, add a splash of brandy to the hot chocolate.

To make the churros, put the milk, water, butter and sugar into a saucepan, set over a medium heat and gradually bring to the boil. Remove from the heat, add the salt and flour and beat vigorously with a wooden spoon. Return to the heat and cook for 2–3 minutes, stirring constantly, until the mixture is thick and starts to come away from the sides of the pan. Remove from the heat and tip into a large bowl.

Using a balloon whisk, beat in the eggs one at a time until the mixture is smooth and glossy. Spoon the mix into a piping bag fitted with a small star nozzle. Chill for 2 hours until firm.

Meanwhile, make the hot chocolate: put all the ingredients in a saucepan and set over a low heat, stirring continuously until the chocolate and sugar have melted. Set aside and reheat gently before serving.

Heat the oil for deep-frying to 180°C (350°F). Check to see if the oil is hot enough (see page 226). When the oil is ready, pipe 7–10 cm (3–4 inch) lengths of the dough into the oil, using scissors to snip off the pieces. Fry for 2–3 minutes until golden brown and puffed up. You will need to do this in batches to stop the churros from overcrowding the oil and sticking together. Drain the churros on kitchen paper, sprinkle with caster sugar and serve with the hot chocolate.

Growing up, I remember my mum making these as a treat… I also remember stopping at service stations on long journeys, either at a Happy Eater or Little Chef, and these sundaes being the only thing on the menu that actually looked exactly like the picture when you ordered it! I still think they are a kids' favourite – what's not to like? Plus, children can make them themselves, layering what they want to put in, so getting them involved and excited in the process. Only one stipulation in my house – it HAS to have a cherry on top!

Classic knickerbocker glory

SERVES 4

1 x 135 g packet strawberry jelly

12 peach slices

12 strawberries, hulled and quartered

8 scoops of vanilla ice cream

200 ml (7 fl oz) whipped or squirty cream

ready-made chocolate and strawberry sauce, for drizzling

4 tablespoons chopped hazelnuts

4 glacé or maraschino cherries

Make up the jelly according to the packet instructions and refrigerate to set (or use ready-made).

Get 4 tall glasses and start layering the ingredients: a spoonful of set jelly, then a peach slice, a couple of strawberries, then a scoop of ice cream and then layer again.

Top with the whipped or squirty cream, chocolate and strawberry sauce, chopped hazelnuts… and finish with a cherry on top!

I am not a fan of milk – I have a teaspoonful in my tea and hate cereal because of it, but one thing I love is milk jelly. My mum used to make strawberry blancmange as a pudding when she couldn't think of anything else to do, and the creamy strawberry, almost milkshake flavour is really comforting to me. She used to serve it in a retro rabbit-shaped mould, and being a sucker for tradition I do the same for Billie and her friends, too!

Strawberry blancmange

SERVES 4—6

8 gelatine leaves

800 g (1 lb 10 oz) strawberries, hulled and chopped

100 g (3½ oz) icing sugar

300 ml (½ pint) full-fat milk

400 ml (14 fl oz) double cream

Place the gelatine leaves in a bowl of iced water and leave to soak for 5 minutes.

Put the strawberries into a saucepan with the icing sugar, bring to the boil then simmer over a medium-high heat for 10 minutes. Remove from the heat and pour the mixture into a fine sieve set over a bowl. Leave the juice to drip through the sieve. You can push it through with the back of a ladle but don't press too hard; you want to avoid getting any strawberry seeds in the liquid.

Measure the liquid; you need 300 ml (½ pint) for the blancmange but any leftover can be used as a delicious strawberry coulis.

Pour the milk and cream into a saucepan and warm gently; it should be just hot but not simmering. Remove from the heat and stir in the strawberry juice. Squeeze the water from the gelatine leaves and stir into the strawberry mixture.

Pour the mixture into a 1 litre (1¾ pint) jelly mould or bowl and transfer to the fridge to set for 4 hours, or overnight if possible.

When the blancmange has set, fill a large container (or the kitchen sink) with hot water and carefully lower the mould in. Hold for a few seconds, then turn out on to a serving plate. Serve on its own or with fresh strawberries and some lightly whipped cream.

I vividly remember this cake from my childhood. The lady who lived across the road from us made a mean fridge cake, really chocolatey and buttery with crunchy biscuits and raisins. I have substituted sour cherries for raisins because they are my favourite, but the great thing about this is that you can put whatever you want in it. I also like to set it in a loaf tin so that you get those lovely hard slices of chocolate heaven!

Fridge cake

SERVES 6—8

50 g (2 oz) dark chocolate
50 g (2 oz) milk chocolate
100 g (3½ oz) salted butter
2 tablespoons golden syrup
150 g (5 oz) digestive biscuits
25 g (1 oz) sour cherries
15 g (½ oz) Rice Krispies

Melt the chocolate, butter and syrup together in a bain-marie.

Smash the biscuits a little and chop the cherries. Combine all the ingredients together in a bowl.

Line a loaf tin with cling film and press the mixture into it. Leave to set in the fridge for a few hours before cutting into slices to serve.

My favourite book is Like Water For Chocolate by Laura Esquivel. It is the most beautiful story of love, passion and food and each chapter begins with a recipe. I first read this book in 1992 and the Cream Fritters sounded so delicious I had a go at making them. Years later and I still love them – the aroma of really sweet fried custard reminds me of the smell of hot donuts at funfairs. I have tried many different recipes over the years, but this seems to work the best.

Fried custard triangles

MAKES 12

1 litre (1¾ pints) whole milk

a pinch of saffron threads

1 vanilla pod

8 egg yolks

125 g (4 oz) caster sugar, plus extra for sprinkling

40 g (1½ oz) plain flour

25 g (1 oz) cornflour

2 tablespoons vegetable oil

25 g (1 oz) unsalted butter

Note: These are delicious served with a sharp rhubarb compote.

Pour the milk into a large saucepan and add the saffron. Split the vanilla pod, scrape the seeds into the saucepan and drop in the pod. Set over a high heat and bring to just below boiling point. Remove from the heat and set aside.

Whisk the egg yolks and sugar together in a large bowl until pale and then whisk in the flour and cornflour.

Strain the hot milk through a sieve into a clean saucepan. Pour half of the milk on to the egg yolk mixture, whisk to combine and then pour it back into the saucepan with the remaining milk. Bring to the boil and cook for 2 minutes, stirring constantly – the mixture will thicken very quickly so make sure you keep stirring and scraping the bottom of the pan. Reduce the heat and cook for a further 5 minutes. Remove from the heat.

Line a 24 x 18 cm (9½ x 7 inch) deep non-stick tin with cling film and pour in the thick custard mixture. Press a sheet of cling film on top of the mixture then transfer to the fridge for 2 hours or until firm.

Turn the set custard out on to a chopping board, peel off the cling film and cut into 12 triangles or squares.

Heat the oil and butter in a frying pan until foaming and then fry the custard triangles or squares in batches for about 2 minutes on each side until golden brown. Drain on kitchen paper then sprinkle with caster sugar. Serve warm.

When I was little we made butterfly cakes all the time. My mum would often whip them up for a cake sale. I used to think it was so clever how everything seemed to fit properly and make a perfect butterfly.

I love white chocolate and I love brownies, so heaven to me is a white chocolate brownie... or, as they are aptly named, blondies! I serve these with the $5 milkshake; I got the idea from *Pulp Fiction*, one of my favourite films. Not exactly a child-friendly movie, but the shake is deeeelicious!

Blondies and $5 shake

MAKES ABOUT 12 BLONDIES
AND 4 SHAKES

100 g (3½ oz) white chocolate, broken into pieces

100 g (3½ oz) butter

2 eggs

250 g (9 oz) caster sugar

125 g (4 oz) plain flour

a pinch of salt

1 teaspoon baking powder

FOR THE $5 SHAKE

3 vanilla pods, split and seeds scraped

500 ml (17 fl oz) whole milk

3 generous scoops best-quality vanilla ice cream

1 tablespoon malted drink powder, plus extra for dusting

4 maraschino cherries

Note: What separates a brownie/blondie from a cake is its gooey consistency, so be careful not to overcook. It needs to have the golden, almost crispy top, but with a 'squidgy wobble' underneath.

Preheat the oven to 180°C (350°F), gas mark 4 and grease and line a 26 x 20 cm (10½ x 8 inch) baking tray.

Melt 70 g (2¾ oz) of the white chocolate and the butter in a bain-marie.

Whisk the eggs and sugar together in a large bowl until pale. Fold in the buttery chocolate mixture and then fold in the flour, salt and baking powder. Chop the remaining chocolate and add this to the mixture. Stir to combine.

Pour the mixture into the prepared baking tray and cook in the preheated oven for 20–25 minutes. Turn out on to a wire rack to cool and then cut into squares.

To make the milkshake, tip the vanilla seeds, milk, ice cream and malted drink powder into a food processor or blender and blitz until smooth and frothy. Divide between 4 tall glasses and dust each one with a little malted drink powder. Top each with a cherry and serve with the blondies.

When I was little we made these cakes all the time. My mum would often whip them up for a cake sale or Brownies' jumble sale. I used to think it was so clever how she seemed to always get an exact circle and that everything seemed to fit properly and make a perfect butterfly, but I see now when making these with Billie that they are so easy and pretty foolproof! With so many different coloured icings and sparkles about, you can decorate these really flamboyantly but, as a creature of habit and comfort, I like mine with good old-fashioned butter icing and strawberry jam.

Butterfly cakes

MAKES ABOUT 12 CAKES
100 g (3½ oz) butter
100 g (3½ oz) caster sugar
2 eggs, beaten
1 teaspoon vanilla extract
100 g (3½ oz) self-raising flour
strawberry or raspberry jam, for the topping

FOR THE BUTTERCREAM ICING
150 g (5 oz) unsalted butter
300 g (10 oz) icing sugar
1–2 tablespoons milk

Preheat the oven to 180°C (350°F), gas mark 4. Line a baking tray with 12 paper fairy cake cases.

Put the butter in a large bowl and beat by hand or with an electric hand-held whisk until pale – this is a tip I was taught while learning to make cupcakes at the Magnolia Bakery in New York. Add the sugar and beat until pale and fluffy.

Add the eggs a little at a time and then the vanilla extract. Fold in the flour with a metal spoon.

Spoon the mixture into the cases and bake in the preheated oven for 12–15 minutes. Cool on a wire rack.

Meanwhile, make the icing by beating the butter in a large bowl until creamy, then sift in the icing sugar and whisk until combined. Add the milk and mix until smooth, adding more if necessary.

To assemble the cakes, cut a small circle off the top of each cake and then cut the circle in half. Spoon a little buttercream into the hole and stick the 2 halves either side to look like wings. Spread a little of the jam on top of the buttercream.

This is my niece Lola's recipe, so who better than her to tell the story:

'My friend and I used to walk to school together, making sure we passed the bakery to buy some gingerbread men for break time. One day she came to my house after school and we were bored and so decided to make our own "gingeys". Since then Eva-Rose (my sister) and I make them all the time, spending hours decorating them with different outfits using different coloured icing, making all the members of the family!'

Lola's gingerbread men

MAKES ABOUT 18 USING A
LARGE GINGERBREAD MAN
CUTTER

1½ teaspoons ground ginger

**350 g (11½ oz) plain flour, plus
extra for dusting**

125 g (4 oz) unsalted butter

1 teaspoon bicarbonate of soda

1 egg

175 g (6 oz) soft brown sugar

6 tablespoons golden syrup

Preheat the oven to 180°C (350°F), gas mark 4. Grease 2–3 baking trays, depending on size.

Put the ground ginger, flour, butter and bicarbonate of soda in a mixing bowl.

Mix it all together using your fingers until it resembles breadcrumbs.

Add the egg, sugar and 4 tablespoons of the syrup and then mix again using your fingers, until it looks like pastry. At this point I add 2 more tablespoons of syrup to enable the mixture to bind together.

Dust a work surface with flour and roll out the pastry to about 5 mm (¼ inch) thick, using a rolling pin. Cut out the gingerbread shapes with a cutter and place them on the greased baking trays.

Bake in the preheated oven for 10 minutes until golden. Leave to cool and then decorate with icing, chocolate chips and various other toppings of your choice.

Index

Thank you

First of all to the 'A team': Chris Terry, Danny, Miranda, Polly, Justine, SuperRich and my wonderful Nicky for the happiest days working on this. You all rock!

To my sister Victoria, as always my voice of reason and reality, and again being my editor. Fancy a job??

To my Billie – my dream, my inspiration, my reason.

To John Douglas – I cannot thank you enough for your help, support, notes, talk, friendship, true kindness and proper proper inspiration. Puppets and Marionettes.

To my family of all sorts: Lola, Eva-Rose, Jonny, Allen, Stacks, Nanna, Tallulah, Missy, Esme, Iris, Angie, Nicnic, Posh and Jasee, Em and DanDan, Ant Sue, Nina, Pat and Ann. To my wonderful Daddy, and Cheryl.

To all who helped, talked, and gave and cooked recipes: Pixie Prince Dhruv, Nikki Morgan, my delicious Lizzie, Chrissie Chung, Paul Hollywood, Patrick Ryan, Steve Groves, Tom Kitchin, The Ace Matt Tebbutt, Mark Sargeant, Eric Lanlard, DanDan, Stevie G, Pixie Holly, John 'show husband' Gilbert and Miss Katie Attwood.

To my truly brilliant agent, friend and conqueror of the world, Jonny McWilliams.

To the best PR in the land and again my true friend, Lou Plank.

To my lovely literary agent Jonathan Conway.

To the brilliant team at Simon & Schuster: Kerr, Ami, Nicky (again!) and Lovely Nigel – you are all so truly supportive and, as I've said before, 'get me'.

To my inspiration from above: Mummy, Betty, Norman and my Lely.

And to everyone who has supported me and bought my first book. Twitter followers, you rock!

Love, and cook the way YOU cook!

Lisa xxx

For more information on Patrick Ryan's new bread school, The Firehouse Bakery and Bread School (www.thefirehouse.ie).

The publishers would also like to thank Stoves, Kitchenaid, Magimix, Kin Knives, Clinique, Dermalogica and Smashbox Cosmetics.

Props: Lou Rota (www.lourota.com).